AA

Portuguese

phrase book

AA Publishing

Contents

English edition prepared by First Edition Translations Ltd, Great Britain

Designed and produced by AA Publishing

First published in 1995 as Wat & Hoe Portugees,

Van Dale Lexicografie bv - Utrecht/Antwerpen

Reprinted May 1999
Reprinted Feb and Sep 2000
Reprinted May 2001
Reprinted Aug 2002
Reprinted Dec 2003

A CIP catalogue record for this book is available from the British Library

Published by AA Publishing (a trading name of Automobile Association Developments Limited, whose registered office is Millstream, Maidenhead Road, Windsor, Berkshire SL4 5GD.
Registered number 1878835)

A01978

Typeset by Anton Graphics Ltd, Andover, Hampshire.

Printed and bound by G. Canale C.SpA, Torino, Italy.

Find out more about AA Publishing and the wide range of services the AA provides by visiting our web site at www.theAA.com

Introduction

Welcome to the AA's new Essential Phrase Books series, covering the most popular European languages and containing everything you'd expect from a comprehensive language series. They're concise, accessible and easy to understand, and you'll find them indispensable on your trip abroad.

Each guide is divided into 15 themed sections and starts with a pronunciation table which gives you the phonetic spelling to all the words and phrases you'll need to know for your trip, while at the back of the book is an extensive word list and grammar guide which will help you construct basic sentences in your chosen language.

Throughout the book you'll come across coloured boxes with a beside them. These are designed to help you if you can't understand what your listener is saying to you. Hand the book over to them and encourage them to point to the appropriate answer to the question you are asking.

Other coloured boxes in the book - this time without the symbol - give alphabetical listings of themed words with their English translations beside them.

For extra clarity, we have put all English words and phrases in black, foreign language terms in red and their phonetic pronunciation in italic.

This phrase book covers all subjects you are likely to come across during the course of your visit, from reserving a room for the night to ordering food and drink at a restaurant and what to do if your car breaks down or you lose your traveller's cheques and money. With over 2,000 commonly used words and essential phrases at your fingertips you can rest assured that you will be able to get by in all situations, so let the Essential Phrase Book become your passport to a secure and enjoyable trip!

Pronunciation table

English speakers can imitate the actual sound of the words by saying the version in italics. Correctly placed stress is essential:
Words ending in a vowel or in **m** or **s** are usually stressed on the penultimate syllable, for example:

o rato	*(oo rah-too)*	the mouse

Words that end in a consonant other than **m** or **s** are stressed on the last syllable e.g. ***cruel*** (*croo-ell*) - cruel, and exceptions to the rule are words marked with an accent, for example, ***falência*** (bankruptcy). Emphasised nasal pronunciation is indicated by the til accent (~), for example, ***nações*** *(nations).*

Vowels

ã	pronounced approximately as in **sung** (***irmã***)
ão	pronounced as **ow** in **howl** (***limão***)
final **e**	barely pronounced (***onde***)
ê	as in **they** (***relê)***
es	***sh*** as in **Estoril** (*shtooreel)*
final **o**	as in **loop** (***macaco***)
ô	as in **local** (***vôo****)*
u	as in **rule**, and silent in ***gue, gui, que*** and ***qui***

Consonants

ç	as in **receive**, e.g. ***laço***
ch	as in **shock**, e.g. ***choque***
h	always silent, e.g. ***hora***
lh	as **ll** in **million**, e.g. ***milhão***
nh	as **ni** in **onion**, e.g. ***linha***
qu	before **e** or **i** pronounced as in **kick**, e.g. ***quilo***; before **a** or **o** pronounced as in **quote**, e.g. ***qualidade***
r	always trilled
-s-	before **b**, **d**, **g**, **l**, **m**, **n**, **r** and **v**, as in **leisure** e.g. ***rasgo***
-s-, -s	before **c**, **f**, **p**, **qu**, **t** and when it is the last letter, with a **sh** sound as in **sugar**, e.g. ***respeito***
x	initial or before a consonant as pronounced as in **sugar**, e.g. ***xícara***; in **ex** pronounced as in **squeeze**, e.g. ***exemplo***
z	when in final position, as in **leisure**, e.g. ***conduz,*** otherwise like an ordinary z

1

Useful lists

1 Useful lists

1.1 Today or tomorrow?

What day is it today?	Que dia é hoje? *kuh deeah eh oarje?*
Today's Monday	Hoje é segunda-feira *oarje eh segunda-fayrah*
– Tuesday	Hoje é terça-feira *oarje eh tearsah-fayrah*
– Wednesday	Hoje é quarta-feira *oarje eh cuartah-fayrah*
– Thursday	Hoje é quinta-feira *oarje eh keentah-fayrah*
– Friday	Hoje é sexta-feira *oarje eh seshtah-fayrah*
– Saturday	Hoje é sábado *oarje eh sarbadoo*
– Sunday	Hoje é domingo *oarje eh doomeengoo*
in January	em Janeiro *ey janayroo*
since February	desde Fevereiro *desduh fevverayroo*
in spring	na primavera *nuh preemaverrah*
in summer	no verão *noo verau*
in autumn	no outono *noo ohtohnoo*
in winter	no inverno *noo invairnoo*
1997	mil novecentos e noventa e sete *meel novsentush ee nooventa ee set*
the twentieth century	o século XX (vinte) *oo seckooloo veent*
What's the date today?	Que dia é hoje? *kuh deeah eh oarje*
Today's the 24th	Hoje é dia vinte e quatro *oarje eh deeah veent ee cuartroo*
Monday, November 2nd, 1998	segunda feira, dois de Novembro de 1998 *segunda fayrah, doysh duh novembroo duh meel novsentush ee novventa ee aytoo*
in the morning	de manhã *duh manyair*
in the afternoon	de tarde *duh tard*
in the evening	à noite *ah noyt*
at night	de noite *duh noyt*
this morning	hoje de manhã *oarje duh manyair*
this afternoon	hoje à tarde *oarje ah tard*

this evening	hoje à noite *oarje ah noyt*
tonight	esta noite *eshta noyt*
last night	na noite passada *nah noyt passada*
this week	esta semana *eshta semarnah*
next month	no próximo mês *noo prossimoo mayge*
last year	no ano passado *noo arnoo passardoo*
next...	no próximo... *noo prosseemoo...*
in...days/weeks/ months/years	daqui a...dias/semanas/meses/anos *dakee ah...deeash/semarnash/mayzesh/ arnoosh*
...weeks ago	hã...semanas *ah...semarnash*
day off	feriado *ferriardoo*

1.2 Bank holidays

- **The main public holidays** in Portugal are the following:

January 1	Ano Novo (New Year's Day)
February	Carnaval (Carnival)
March/ April	Sexta-feira Santa (Good Friday)
April 25	Dia da Revolução (Day of the Revolution)
May 1	Dia do Trabalhador (Labour Day)
June 10	Dia de Portugal (Camões Day commemorating Portugal's equivalent to Shakespeare)
June 13	Santo António (Festival of St. Anthony, patron saint of Lisbon)
June 24	São João (Festival of St. John, celebrated in Oporto and the North)
August 15	Assunção da Nossa Senhora (Feast of the Assumption)
October 5	Dia da República (Republic Day)
November 1	Dia de Todos os Santos (All Saints Day)
December 1	Restauração da Independência (Restoration Day)
December 8	Imaculada Conceição (Feast of the Immaculate Conception)
December 25	Dio da Nata (Christmas Day)

Most shops, banks and government departments are closed on these days.
Boxing Day is not a public holiday.

1.3 What time is it?

What time is it?	Que horas são? *kay oarash sow?*
It's nine o'clock	São nove horas *sow nov oarash*
– five past ten	São dez e cinco *sow dez ee seenkoo*

– a quarter past eleven	São onze e um quarto *sow onz ee oom cuartoo*
– twenty past twelve	É meio dia e vinte *eh mayoo deeah ee veent*
– half past one	É uma e meia *eh oomah ee mayah*
– twenty-five to three	São três menos vinte e cinco *sow trayge mennush veent ee seenkoo*
– a quarter to four	São quatro menos um quarto *sow cuartroo mennush oom cuartoo*
– ten to five	São cinco menos dez *sow seenkoo mennush dej/*
– twelve noon	É meio dia *eh mayoo deeah*
– midnight	É meia noite *eh mayah noyt*
half an hour	uma meia hora *oomah mayah orah*
What time?	A que horas? *ah kay orash?*
What time can I come round?	A que horas é que posso ir? *ah kay orash eh kuh possoo eer?*
At...	Às... *ush...*
After...	Depois das... *depoysh dush...*
Before...	Antes das... *antesh dush...*
Between...and...	Entre as...e as... *entrash...ee ush...*
From...to...	Das...às... *dush...ush*
In...minutes	Daqui a...minutos *dakee uh...minootoosh*
– an hour	Daqui a uma hora *dakee uh ooma ora*
– ...hours	Daqui a...horas *dakee uh...orash*
– a quarter of an hour	Daqui a um quarto de hora *dakee ah oom cuartoo dora*
– three quarters of an hour	Daqui a três quartos de hora *dakee ah trayge cuartoosh dora*
early/late	cedo/tarde *sedoo/tard*
on time	a horas *uh orash*
summertime	horário de verão *oraryoo duh verau*
wintertime	horário de inverno *orarioo duh invairnoo*

1.4 One, two, three...

0	zero	*zairoo*
1	um	*oom*
2	dois	*doysh*
3	três	*trayge*

4	quatro	*cuartroo*
5	cinco	*seenkoo*
6	seis	*saysh*
7	sete	*set*
8	oito	*oytoo*
9	nove	*nov*
10	dez	*dej*
11	onze	*onz*
12	doze	*doaze*
13	treze	*treyze*
14	catorze	*cattorz*
15	quinze	*keenze*
16	dezasseis	*dezzasaysh*
17	dezassete	*dezzaset*
18	dezoito	*dezzoytoo*
19	dezanove	*dezzanov*
20	vinte	*veent*
21	vinte e um	*veenty oom*
22	vinte e dois	*veenty doysh*
30	trinta	*treenta*
31	trinta e um	*treenty oom*
32	trinta e dois	*treenty doysh*
40	quarenta	*cuarenta*
50	cinquenta	*seencuenta*
60	sessenta	*sessenta*
70	setenta	*settenta*
80	oitenta	*oytenta*
90	noventa	*nooventa*
100	cem	*same*
101	cento e um	*sentoo ee oom*
110	cento e dez	*sentoo ee dej*
120	cento e vinte	*sentoo ee veent*
200	duzentos	*doozentoosh*
300	trezentos	*trayzentoosh*
400	quatrocentos	*cuartroosentoosh*
500	quinhentos	*keenyentush*
600	seiscentos	*sayshsentoosh*
700	setecentos	*setsentoosh*
800	oitocentos	*oytsentoosh*
900	novecentos	*novsentoosh*
1000	mil	*meel*
1100	mil e cem	*meely same*
2000	dois mil	*doysh meel*
10,000	dez mil	*dej meel*
100,000	cem mil	*say meel*
1,000,000	milhão	*meelyau*

1st	primeiro	*preemayroo*
2nd	segundo	*seggoondoo*
3rd	terceiro	*tairsayroo*
4th	quarto	*cuartoo*
5th	quinto	*keentoo*
6th	sexto	*seshtoo*
7th	sétimo	*settimoo*
8th	oitavo	*oytahvoo*
9th	nono	*nohnoo*
10th	décimo	*dessimoo*

11th	décimo primeiro	*dessimoo preemayroo*
12th	décimo segundo	*dessimoo segundoo*
13th	décimo terceiro	*dessimoo tairsayroo*
14th	décimo quarto	*dessimoo cuartoo*
15th	décimo quinto	*dessimoo keentoo*
16th	décimo sexto	*dessimoo seshtoo*
17th	décimo sétimo	*dessimoo settimoo*
18th	décimo oitavo	*dessimoo oytarvoo*
19th	décimo nono	*dessimoo nohnoo*
20th	vigésimo	*veejezimoo*
21st	vigésimo primeiro	*veejezimoo preemayroo*
22nd	vigésimo segundo	*veejezimoo segoondoo*
30th	trigésimo	*treejezimoo*
100th	centésimo	*sentezimoo*
1000th	milésimo	*milezimoo*

once	uma vez *ooma vayzh*
twice	duas vezes *dooash vayzesh*
double	o dobro *oo dobroo*
triple	o triplo *oo treeploo*
half	a metade *uh mettard*
a quarter	um quarto *oom cuartoo*
a third	um terço *oom tairsoo*
a couple, a few, some	um par de, uns, alguns *oom par duh, oonsh, algoomash*
2+4=6	dois mais quatro são seis *doysh mysh cuartroo sow saysh*
4-2=2	quatro menos dois são dois *cuartroo mennush doysh sow doysh*
2x4=8	dois vezes quatro são oito *dooash vayzesh cuartroo sow oytoo*
4÷2=2	quatro a dividir por dois são dois *cuartroo uh divvideer por doysh sow doysh*
odd/even	par/ímpar *par/eempar*
total	(em) total *(aim) tootal*
6x9	seis por nove *saysh por nov*

1.5 The weather

Is the weather going to be good/bad?	Estará bom/mau tempo? *estarah bom tempoo?*
Is it going to get colder/hotter?	Estará mais frio/calor? *estarah mysh freeooh/calore?*
What temperature is it going to be?	Quantos graus vão estar? *cuarntoosh growsh vow eshtar?*
Is it going to rain?	Vai chover? *vy shoover?*

Is there going to be a storm?	Vamos ter uma tempestade? *varmoosh ter ooma tempeshtard?*
Is it going to snow?	Vai nevar? *vy nevvar?*
Is it going to freeze?	Vai haver nevoeiro? *vy aver nevvooayroo?*
Is the thaw setting in?	Vai fazer trovoada? *vy fazzair troovooarda?*
Is it going to be foggy?	O tempo vai mudar? *oo tempoo vy moodar?*
It's cooling down	Vai arrefecer *vy arryfessair*
What's the weather going to be like today/ tomorrow?	Que tempo vamos ter hoje/amanhã? *kuh tempoo varmoosh tair oarje/ahmanyar?*

abafado
muggy
aguaceiro
shower
ameno
mild
bom tempo
fine
céu limpo
clear
céu pouco/muito nublado
light/heavy clouds
(cheio de) sol
sunny
chuva
rain
chuvisco
drizzle
chuvoso
wet
ciclone
hurricane
fresco
cool
frio
cold
gelo
ice
geada
frost
granizo
hail
... graus abaixo/ acima de zero
...degrees above/ below zero
húmido
damp
nebuloso
cloudy
neve
snow
nevoeiro
fog
nublado
overcast
quente
hot
quentíssimo
scorching hot
rajadas de vento
squalls
ruim
bleak
tempestuoso
stormy
trovoada
thunderstorm
vaga de calor
heatwave
vento
wind
vento fraco/ moderado/forte
light/moderate/ strong wind
ventoso
windy

1.6 Here, there...

See also 5.1 Asking for directions

here/there	aqui/ali *akee/alee*
somewhere/nowhere	em algum/nenhum lugar *aim algoom/nenewm loogar*
everywhere	em todo o lado *aim tohdoo oo lardoo*
far away/nearby	longe/perto *lonj/peartoo*
right/left	para a direita/esquerda *parra uh dirrayta/eshkerda*

right/left of	à direita/esquerda de *ah dirrayta/eshkerda duh*
straight ahead	em frente *aim frent*
via	por *poor*
in	em *aim*
on	sobre *sohbre*
under	debaixo de *debyshoo duh*
against	contra *contrah*
opposite	em frente *aim frent*
next to	ao lado de *ow lardoo duh*
near	perto *pairto*
in front of	em frente de *aim frent duh*
in the centre	no centro *noo sentroo*
forward	para diante *parra deeant*
downward	para baixo *parra byshoo*
upward	para cima *parra seema*
inward	para dentro *parra dentroo*
outward	para fora *parra foura*
backward	para trás *parra traj*
at the front	à frente *ah frent*
at the back	atrás *atraj*
in the north	no norte *noo nort*
to the south	para o sul *para oo sool*
from the west	de oeste/do oeste *di esht/doo esti*
from the east	de leste/do leste *duh lesht/doo lesti*
to...from	a...de *ah...duh*

1.7 What does that sign say?

See also 5.4 Traffic signs

aberto/fechado
open/closed
água não potável
not drinking water
alta tensão
high voltage
aluga-se
for hire
avariado/não funciona
out of order
caixa
pay here
completo
full
cuidado com o cão
beware of the dog
cuidado com o degrau
mind the step
é favor não incomodar
do not disturb
elevador
lift
empurre/puxe
push/pull
escada
steps
entrada
entrance
entrada livre/ grátis
entry free
escada de incêndio
fire escape
escada rolante
escalator
homens
gents/gentlemen
horário
opening hours
informações
information
lavabos
toilets
liquidação
clearance
liquidação total
closing-down sale
não mexer
do not touch
passagem/ entrada proibida
no entry
perigo
danger
perigo de incêndio
fire hazard
posto de primeiros socorros
first aid
primeiro andar
first floor
proibida a entrada de animais
no pets allowed
proibido fazer fogueira
no open fires
proibido fotografar
no photographs
proibido fumar
no smoking
proibido pisar a relva
keep off the grass
propriedade privada
private (property)
recepção
reception
reservado
reserved
saída
exit
saída de emergência
emergency exit
saldos
sale
senhoras
ladies
sinal de alarme
alarm signal
tinta fresca
wet paint
vende-se
for sale

1.8 Telephone alphabet

a	*ah*	América	*amereeka*
b	*bay*	Bernardo	*bairnardoo*
c	*say*	Colónia	*colonnia*
d	*day*	Dinamarca	*deenamarca*
e	*eh*	Espanha	*eshpanya*
f	*ef*	França	*fransa*
g	*jey*	Grécia	*gressia*
h	*gar*	Holanda	*ollanda*
i	*ee*	Irlanda	*earlanda*
j	*jotta*	Japão	*japown*
k	*kappa*	Kremlim	*kremleen*
l	*el*	Londres	*londresh*
m	*me*	Madrid	*madree*
n	*ene*	Nápoles	*napolesh*
o	*oh*	Oslo	*ojloo*

p	*peh*	Portugal	*poortoogarl*
q	*q*	Quilo	*keeloo*
r	*err*	Rússia	*roossia*
s	*ess*	Suécia	*swessia*
t	*tay*	Turquia	*toorkeea*
u	*u*	Uruguai	*ooroogwy*
v	*vay*	Vitória	*veetoria*
w	*vay*	Washington	*vasheengton*
x	*sheej*	Xangai	*shangai*
y	*ípsilon*		
z	*zey*	Zurique	*zooreek*

1.9 Personal details

surname	apelido *apelleedoo*
christian name(s)	nome *nom*
initials	iniciais *iniciaish*
address (street/number)	morada (rua/número) *moorada (rua/noomeroo)*
post code/town	código postal *coddigoo pooshtal*
sex (male/female)	sexo (masculino/feminino) *sexoo (mashculeenoo/ femineenoo)*
nationality	nacionalidade *nasseeonalidad*
date of birth	data de nascimento *data duh nashsimentoo*
place of birth	local de nascimento *local duh nashsimentoo*
occupation	profissão *proofissow*
married/single/divorced	casado/solteiro/divorciado *cazadoo/solltayroo/divorciadoo*
widowed	viúva/viúvo *vioova/vioovoo*
(number of) children	(número de) filhos *noomeroo duh feelyoosh*
identity card/passport/ driving licence number	número de bilhete de identidade/ passaporte/carta de condução *noomeroo duh beelyet duh eedentidad/ passaport/carta duh condusow*
place and date of issue	local e data de emissão *loocal ee data duh emissow*

2

Courtesies

2 Courtesies

• **It is usual in Portugal** to shake hands on meeting and parting company. Female friends and relatives may kiss each other on both cheeks when meeting and parting company. With men this varies according to the region.

2.1 Greetings

Hello, Mr Smith	Olá, senhor Smith/Olá, Seu Smith *olah,senyor Smith/olah sayoo Smith*
Hello, Mrs Jones	Olá, Senhora Jones *olah, senyora Jones*
Hello, Peter	Olá, Peter *olah, Peter*
Hi, Helen	Viva, Helen *viva, Helen*
Good morning, madam	Bom dia, minha senhora *bom deeah, meenya senyora*
Good afternoon, sir	Boa tarde, senhor *Boa tard, senyor*
Good evening	boa noite *boa noyt*
Good day	Bom dia *bom deeah*
How are you?	Como está? *comoo eshtah?*
Fine, thank you, and you?	Bem obrigado, e o senhor? *baim obrigahdoo, ee oo senyor?*
Very well	Óptimo *otimoo*
Not very well	Mais ou menos *maiz oh mennush*
Not too bad	Vai se andando *vysuh andandoo*
I'd better be going	Vou andando *vo andandoo*
I have to be going. Someone's waiting for me	Tenho de ir. Estão à minha espera *tenyo duh ear. eshtau uh meenya eshperah*
Goodbye	Tchau! *chau*
See you soon	Adeus! *adayoosh!*
See you later	Até logo! *atay loggoo!*
See you in a little while	Até breve! *atay brev!*
Sleep well	Durma bem *dourma baim*
Goodnight	Boa noite *boa noyt*
All the best	Que tudo lhe corra bem *kuh toodoo lher courrah baim*
Have fun	Divírta-se *deeverts suh*

Good luck	Muita sorte/Boa sorte *muinta sort*
Have a nice holiday	Boas férias *boash ferriash*
Have a good trip	Boa viagem *boa viarjaim*
Thank you, you too	Obrigado, igualmente *obbrigahdoo, eeguarlment*
Say hello to...for me	Dê cumprimentos a... *day coomprimentoosh ah...*

2.2 How to ask a question

Who?	Quem? *kaim?*
Who's that?	Quem é? *kaim eh?*
What?	O quê? *oo kay?*
What's there to see here?	O que é que se pode visitar aqui? *oo kee eh kuh suh pod veesitar akee?*
What kind of hotel is this?	Que tipo de hotel é este? *kuh teepoo di ohtel eh esht?*
Where?	Onde? *ond?*
Where's the toilet?	Onde são os lavabos? *ond sow oosh lavarboosh?*
Where are you going?	Para onde vai? *parra ond vy?*
Where are you from?	De onde é? *di ond eh?*
How?	Como? *commoo?*
How far is that?	A que distância fica? *ah kay dishtancia feeka?*
How long does that take?	Quanto tempo dura? *cuarntoo tempoo doura?*
How long is the trip?	Quanto tempo dura a viagem? *cuarntoo tempoo doura ah veeargaim?*
How much?	Quanto? *cuarntoo?*
How much is this?	Quanto custa isto? *cuarntoo cooshter eeshtoo?*
What time is it?	Que horas são? *kay orash sow?*
Which?	Qual? Quais? *quarl? cwysh?*
Which glass is mine?	Qual é o meu copo? *quarl eh oo mayoo coppoo?*
When?	Quando? *cwarndoo?*
When are you leaving?	Quando é que parte? *cwarndoo eh kuh part?*
Why?	Porquê? *poorkay?*
Could you...me?	Poderia...me? *pooderia...muh?*

Could you help me, please?	Poderia ajudar-me se faz favor? *pooderia ajoodar muh suh faj favor?*
Could you point that out to me?	Poderia indicar-mo? *pooderia eendi-eecar moo?*
Could you come with me, please?	Poderia vir comigo, se faz favor? *pooderia veer comeego, suh faj favor?*
Could you reserve some tickets for me, please?	Poderia reservar-me bilhetes? *pooderia resairvar muh beelyettsh?*
Do you know whether...?	Por acaso, sabe se...? *por acarzoo, sab si...?*
Do you have...?	Tem...? *tame...?*
Do you know another hotel, please?	Conhece outro hotel? *koonyes ohtroo ohtel?*
Could you give me...?	Podia dar-me...? *poodeeah dar muh...?*
Do you have a vegetarian dish, please?	Tem por acaso um prato sem carne? *tame poor acasoo oom prartoo same carn?*
I'd like...	Eu queria... *ew kereeah...*
I'd like a kilo of apples, please.	Eu queria um quilo de maçãs *ew kereeah oom keeloo duh massangsh*
Can I...?	Posso...? *possoo...?*
Can I take this?	Posso levar isto? *possoo levvar eeshtoo?*
Can I smoke here?	Posso fumar aqui? *possoo foomar akee?*
Could I ask you something?	Posso fazer-lhe uma pergunta? *possoo fazzair lhuh ooma pairgoontah?*

2.3 How to reply

Yes, of course	Sim, claro *see, claroo*
No, I'm sorry	Não, desculpe *now, deshcoolp*
Yes, what can I do for you?	Em que posso ser-lhe útil? *aim kuh possoo sair lheh ooteel?*
Just a moment, please	Um momento, se faz favor *oom moomentoo, suh fash favvor*
No, I don't have time now	Não, agora não tenho tempo *now, agorah now tenyoo tempoo*
No, that's impossible	Não, isso é impossível *now, eessoo eh imposseevel*
I think so	Creio que sim *crayoo kuh see*
I agree	Eu também penso que sim *eyoo tambaim pensoo kuh see*
I hope so too	Também o espero *tambaim oo eshpearoo*
No, not at all	Não, de modo nenhum *now, duh mohdoo nenyoom*
No, no one	Não, ninguém *now, ningame*
No, nothing	Não, nada *now, narda*

That's (not) right — Isso está certo (isso está errado)
eesoo eshtah sairtoo (eesoo eshtah errardoo)

I (don't) agree — (Não) estou de acordo/Não concordo consigo
(now) eshtoe di acordoo/now concordoo conseegoo

All right — Está certo
eshtah sairtoo

Okay — De acordo
di acordoo

Perhaps — Talvez
talvayj

I don't know — Não sei
now say

2.4 Thank you

Thank you — Obrigado/muito obrigado
obbrigahdoo/mweentoo obbrigahdoo

You're welcome — De nada/foi um prazer
duh narda/foy oom prahzair

Thank you very much — Muitíssimo obrigado
mweenteessimoo obbrigahdoo

Very kind of you — Muito amável da sua parte
mweentoo amarvel da suah part

I enjoyed it very much — Foi um verdadeiro prazer
foy oom verdadayroo prahzair

Thank you for your trouble — Agradeço-lhe o incómodo
agraddaysoo lhyer oo eencomodoo

You shouldn't have — Não precisava se incomodar
now preceesarva si eencomoodar

That's all right — Não tem de que
now taim duh kay

2.5 Sorry

Sorry! — Perdão
perdow

Excuse me — Com licença
com leesensa

I'm sorry! — Desculpe!
deshcoolp!

I'm sorry, I didn't know... — Desculpe, eu não sabia que ...
deshcoolp, eyoo now sabeeah kuh...

I do apologise — Desculpe-me
deshcoolp muh

I'm sorry — Lamento
lamentoo

I didn't do it on purpose, it was an accident — Não fiz de propósito, foi sem querer
now feej duh propozeetoo, foy same kerrair

That's all right — Não faz mal
now faj mal

Never mind — Deixe lá
daysh la

It could've happened to anyone — Pode acontecer com toda a gente
pod acontessair com toeda ah jent

2.6 What do you think?

What do you think?	O que acha?	*oo keh asha?*
What do you prefer?	O que prefere?	*oo keh prefair?*
Don't you like dancing?	Não gosta de dançar?	*now goshta duh dansar?*
I don't mind	É me indiferente/ Tanto faz	*eh muh eendeeferent/ tantoo faj*
Well done!	Muito bem!	*mueentoo baim!*
Not bad!	Não está mal!	*now eshtah mal!*
Great!	Optimo!	*ottimoo!*
Wonderful!	Que delícia!	*kay delleecia!*
It's really nice here!	Que bem que se está aqui!	*kay baim kuh si eshtah akee!*
How nice!	Que giro/bonito!	*kay geeroo/ booneetoo!*
How nice for you!	Que bom para si!	*kay bom parra see!*
I'm (not) very happy with...	(Não) estou muito contente com...	*(now) eshtoe mweentoo content com...*
I'm glad...	Alegra-me que ...	*allegra muh kuh...*
I'm having a great time	Divirto-me muito	*deeveertoo muh mweentoo*
I'm looking forward to it	Aguardo com muito prazer ...	*agwardoo com mweentoo prazair...*
I hope it'll work out	Espero que dê resultado	*eshpairoo kuh day resultardoo*
That's ridiculous!	Que ridículo!	*kay reedeecooloo!*
That's terrible!	Que terrível!	*kay tereevel!*
What a pity!	Que pena!	*kay pena!*
That's filthy!	Que sujo!	*kay soojoo!*
What a load of rubbish!	Que disparate!	*kay deeshparatt!*
I don't like...	Não gosto de ...	*now goshtoo duh*
I'm bored to death	Aborreço-me terrívelmente	*aboressoo muh terreevelment*
I've had enough	Estou farto/farta	*eshtoe fartoo/ farta*
This is no good	Assim não pode ser	*assee now pod sair*
I was expecting something completely different	Esperava outra coisa completamente diferente	*eshperarvah ohtra coyza completament deeferent*

3

Conversation

3 Conversation

3.1 I beg your pardon?

I don't speak any/ I speak a little...	Não falo/falo um pouco *now faloo/faloo oom poecoo*
I'm English	Sou inglês/inglesa *so inglej/ingleza*
I'm Scottish	Sou escocês/escocesa *so eshcossayj/eshcossayza*
I'm Irish	Sou irlandês/irlandesa *so earlandayj/earlandayza*
I'm Welsh	Sou galês/sou galesa *so gallayj/so gallayza*
Do you speak English/French/German?	Fala inglês/francês/alemão? *fala inglej/fransayj/allaymau?*
Is there anyone who speaks...?	Há alguém que fale...? *ah algaim kuh fal...?*
I beg your pardon?	O que é que diz? *oo kay eh kuh deej?*
I (don't) understand	(Não) compreendo *(now)comprayendoo*
Do you understand me?	Compreende-me? *comprend muh?*
Could you repeat that, please?	Podia repetir se faz favor? *poodeer repeteer suh faj favvor?*
Could you speak more slowly, please?	Podia falar mais devagar? *poodeer falar mysh de-vaggar?*
What does that word mean?	O que significa aquilo/aquela palavra? *oo kuh signifeeka akeeloo/akella pallavra?*
Is that similar to/the same as...?	É (quase) a mesma coisa que...? *eh (quaz) ah mejma coyza kuh...?*
Could you write that down for me, please?	Podia escrever? *poodeer eshcrevair?*
Could you spell that for me, please?	Podia soletrar? *poodeer soolittrar?*
(See 1.8 Telephone alphabet)	
Could you point that out in this phrase book, please?	Podia indicar aqui no guia? *poodeer indeecar akee noo gueea?*
One moment, please, I have to look it up	Um momento, tenho de procurar *oom moomentoo tenyoo duh procurar*
I can't find the word/the sentence	Não encontro a palavra/a frase *now encontroo ah palarvra/ ah frarz*
How do you say that in...?	Como é que se diz em ...? *cohmoo eh kuh suh deej aim...?*
How do you pronounce that?	Como é que se pronuncia? *cohmoo eh kuh suh proonoonsia?*

3.2 Introductions

May I introduce myself?	Posso apresentar-me?	*possoo apprezentar muh?*
My name's...	Chamo-me...	*shamoo muh...*
I'm...	Sou...	*so...*
What's your name?	Como se chama?	*commoo suh shamma?*
May I introduce...?	Apresento lhe...	*aprezentoo lhya...*
– my wife/ daughter/ mother/girlfriend	A minha mulher/filha/mãe/amiga	*uh meenya moolyer/feelya/ameega*
– my husband/son/ father/boyfriend	O meu marido/filho/pai/amigo	*oo mayoo mareedoo/feelyoo/ameegoo*
How do you do	Muito prazer em conhecê-lo	*mueentoo prazair aim coonyessay loo*
Pleased to meet you	Muito prazer (em conhecê-lo)	*mueentoo prazair aim coonyessay loo*
Where are you from?	Donde é?/De onde é?	*dond eh?/di ondi eh?*
I'm from England/Scotland/Ireland/ Wales	Sou da Inglaterra/Escócia/Irlanda/Gales	*so da eenglatera/eshcossia/eerlanda/garlesh*
What city do you live in?	Em que cidade mora?	*aim kay sidard mora?*
In... It's near...	Em... É perto de...	*aim... eh pairtoo duh*
Have you been here long?	Já está cá há muito tempo?	*jah eshtah cah hah mweentoo tempoo?*
A few days	Há uns dias	*ha unsh deeash*
How long are you staying here?	Quanto tempo fica cá?	*cuarntoo tempoo feeka cah?*
We're (probably) leaving tomorrow/in two weeks	Partimos (provavelmente) amanhã/daqui a duas semanas	*partimoosh (proovarvelment) armanyar/dakee ah dooash semarnash*
Where are you staying?	Onde está hospedado?	*ond eshtah oshpedardoo?*
In a hotel/an apartment	Num hotel/apartamento	*noom ohtel/ apartarmentoo*
On a camp site	Num parque de campismo	*noom park duh campeejmoo*
With friends/relatives	Em casa de uns amigos/familiares	*aim carza di uns amigoosh/familiaresh*
Are you here on your own/with your family?	Está cá sozinho/com a família?	*eshtah cah sozeenyoo/com ah fameelya?*
I'm on my own	Estou sozinho	*eshtoe sozeenyoo*
I'm with my partner/wife/husband	Estou com a minha amiga/o meu amigo/a minha mulher/o meu marido	*eshtoe com ah meenya ameega/oo mayoo ameegoo/ah meenya mullyer/oo mayoo mareedoo*

– with my family	Estou com a minha família *eshtoe com ah meenya fameelya*
– with relatives	Estou com familiares *eshtoe com familiaresh*
– with a friend/friends	Estou com um amigo/uma amiga/amigos *eshtoe com oom ameegoo/ooma ameega/ ameegoosh*
Are you married?	É casado/casada? *eh cazardo/cazarda*
Do you have a steady boyfriend/girlfriend?	Tens namorado/namorada? *taynsh namorardoo/namorardah?*
That's none of your business	Não tem nada com isso *now taim narda com eesoo*
I'm married	Sou casado/casada *so cazardo/cazarda*
– single	Sou solteiro/solteira *so soltayroo/soltayrah*
– separated	Estou separado/separada *eshtoe separardoo/separardah*
– divorced	Estou divorciado/divorciada *eshtoe deevorciardoo/deevorciardah*
– a widow/widower	Sou viúva/viúvo *so veeoova/veeoovoo*
I live alone/with someone	Vivo sozinho/com um companheiro *veevoo sozzeenyoo/com oom companyayroo*
Do you have any children/grandchildren?	Tem filhos/netos? *taim feelyoosh/nettoosh?*
How old are you?	Que idade tem? *kuh eedad taim?*
How old is she/he?	Que idade tem ela/ele? *kuh eedad taim ella/el?*
I'm...	Tenho...anos *tenyo...anoosh*
She's/he's...	Ela/ele tem...anos *ella/el taim...anoosh*
What do you do for a living?	O que é que faz? *oo kay eh kuh faj?*
I work in an office	Trabalho num escritório *trabalyoo noom eshcritoryoo*
I'm a student/ I'm at school	Estudo/ando na escola *eshtoodoo/andoo nah eshcolla*
I'm unemployed	Estou desempregado *eshtoe dezempregardoo*
I'm retired	Estou reformado *eshtoe refformardoo*
I'm on a disability pension	Estou reformado por causa de inválidez *eshtoe refformardoo por cowza di eenvallidesh*
I'm a housewife	Sou dona de casa *so donna duh carza*
Do you like your job?	Gosta do seu trabalho? *goshta doo sayoo trabalyoo?*
Most of the time	Às vezes sim, às vezes não *aj vaizesh see, aj vaizesh now*
I usually do, but I prefer holidays	Geralmente sim, mas gosto mais de férias *jerarlment si maj goshtoo mysh duh ferriash*

3.3 Starting/ending a conversation

Could I ask you something?	Posso fazer-lhe uma pergunta? *possoo fazer lyer ooma pergoontah*
Excuse me	Desculpe *deshcoolp*
Excuse me, could you help me?	Desculpe, podia ajudar-me? *deshcoolp poodeer ajoodar muh?*
Yes, what's the problem?	Sim, o que é? *see oo kee eh?*
What can I do for you?	O que deseja? *oo kuh dezayjah?*
Sorry, I don't have time now	Desculpe, agora não tenho tempo *deshcoolp agorah now tenyoo tempoo*
Do you have a light?	Tem lume? *taim loom?*
May I join you?	Posso sentar-me ao seu lado? *possoo sentar muh ow sayoo lardoo?*
Could you take a picture of me/us? Press this button	Podia tirar-me/tirar-nos uma fotografia? Carregue neste botão. *podia tirrar muh/tirrar nooz ooma fotografffia? carreg nesht bootau*
Leave me alone	Deixe-me em paz *daysh muh aim paj*
Get lost	Vá-se embora! *vah suh emborah!*
Go away or I'll scream	Se não se for embora, começo a gritar! *suh now suh for emborah comessoo ah greetarr!*

3.4 Congratulations and condolences

Happy birthday/many happy returns	Feliz aniversário! *feleej annivaisaryoo!*
Please accept my condolences	Os meus pêsames *oosh mayoosh pezamesh*
I'm very sorry for you	Sinto muito *seentoo mueentoo*

3.5 A chat about the weather

See also 1.5 The weather

It's so hot/cold today!	Que calor/frio está hoje! *kay calorr/freeyoo eshtah oarje!*
Nice weather, isn't it?	Que bom tempo! *kay bom tempoo!*
What a wind/storm!	Que vento/tempestade! *kay ventoo/tempeshtad!*
All that rain/snow!	Que chuva/neve! *kay choova/nev!*
All that fog!	Que nevoeiro! *kay nevooayroo!*
Has the weather been like this for long here?	O tempo já está assim há muitos dias? *oo tempoo jah eshtah aseem ah mueentoosh deeash?*

Is it always this hot/cold here?	**Aqui está sempre tanto calor/frio?** *akee eshtah semprah tantoo calor/freeyoo?*
Is it always this dry/wet here?	**Aqui o tempo está sempre tão seco/húmido?** *akee oo tempoo eshtah semprah tau saycoo/oomidoo?*

3.6 Hobbies

Do you have any hobbies?	**Tem algum passatempo?** *taim algoom passatempoo?*
I like painting/reading/photography/DIY	**Gosto de pintar/ler/fotografar/biscates** *gostoo duh peentar/lair/fotoggrafar/beeshcatsh*
I like music	**Gosto de música** *goshtoo duh moosica*
I like playing the guitar/piano	**Gosto de tocar guitarra/piano** *goshtoo duh toocar guitarra/ pianoo*
I like going to the movies	**Gosto de ir ao cinema** *goshtoo duh ir ow cinaymah*
I like travelling/sport/fishing/walking	**Gosto de viajar/fazer desporto/pescar/passear** *goshtoo duh veeajar/fazair deshportoo/passeear*

3.7 Being the host(ess)

See also 4 Eating out

Can I offer you a drink?	**Posso oferecer-lhe uma bebida?** *possoo offeressair lya ooma bebbeeda?*
What would you like to drink?	**O que é que queres beber?** *oo kee eh kuh cairesh bebbair?*
Something non-alcoholic, please	**Preferia uma bebida não alcoólica** *prefferia ooma bebbeeda now alcoohollica*
Would you like a cigarette/cigar/to roll your own?	**Quer um cigarro/charuto/cigarro de enrolar?** *care oom cigaroo/sharootoo/cigaroo duh enroolar?*
I don't smoke	**Não fumo** *now foomoo*

3.8 Invitations

Are you doing anything tonight?	**Vais fazer alguma coisa esta noite?** *vysh fazzair algooma coyza eshta noyt?*
Do you have any plans for today/this afternoon/tonight?	**Já tem planos para hoje/esta tarde/hoje à noite?** *jah taim planoosh parra oarje/eshta tard/oarje ah noyt?*
Would you like to go out with me?	**Gostaria de sair comigo?** *goshtareeah duh syeer commeegoo?*
Would you like to go dancing with me?	**Quer dançar comigo?** *care dansar commeegoo?*
Would you like to have lunch/dinner with me?	**Quer almoçar/jantar comigo?** *care almoosar/jantar commeegoo?*

Would you like to come to the beach with me?	Quer ir à praia comigo? *care eer ah prya commeegoo?*
Would you like to come into town with us?	Quer ir ao centro connosco? *care eer ow sentroo conoshcoo?*
Would you like to come and see some friends with us?	Quer ir a casa de uns amigos connosco? *care eer ah carza di unsh ameegoosh conoshcoo?*
Shall we dance?	Vamos dançar? *varmoosh dansar?*
– sit at the bar?	Vámonos sentar no bar? *vamoo noosh sentar noo bar?*
– get something to drink?	Vámos beber qualquer coisa? *varmoosh bebbair qualcair coyza?*
– go for a walk/drive?	Vámos dar uma volta a pé/de carro? *varmoosh dar ooma vollta ah peh/duh cahroo?*
Yes, all right	Sim, está bem *si eshtah baim*
Good idea	Boa idéia *boa eedaya*
No (thank you)	Não (obrigado) *now obrigardoo*
Maybe later	Talvez logo *talvej loggoo*
I don't feel like it	Não me apetece *now muh aptess*
I don't have time	Não tenho tempo *now tenyoo tempoo*
I already have a date	Já tenho outro encontro *jah tenyoo ohtroo encontroo*
I'm not very good at dancing/volleyball/ swimming	Não sei dançar/jogar voleibol/nadar *now say dansar/joogar volleybol/naddar*

3.9 Paying a compliment

You look wonderful!	Estás com tão bom aspecto! *eshtash com tau bom ashpectoo!*
I like your car!	Que lindo carro! *kuh leendoo cahroo!*
You have beautiful hair	Tens cabelo lindo! *tensh cabayloo leendoo!*
You're a nice boy/girl	És um rapaz amoroso/uma rapariga amorosa *ez oom rappaj amorozzo/ooma rappareega amorozza*
What a sweet child!	Que criança amorosa! *kay creeansa amorozza!*
You're a wonderful dancer!	Danças muito bem! *dansash mweentoo baim!*
You're a wonderful cook!	Cozinhas muito bem! *coozeenyash mweentoo baim!*
You're a terrific soccer player!	Jogas futebol muito bem! *joggash footboll mweentoo baim!*

3 Conversation

3.10 Chatting someone up

I like being with you	Gosto de estar contigo *goshtoo di eshtar conteegoo*
I've missed you so much	Senti muito a tua falta *sentee mweentoo ah tooah falta*
I dreamt about you	Sonhei contigo *sonyay conteegoo*
I think about you all day	Penso o dia inteiro em ti *pensoo oo deeah eentayroo aim tee*
You have such a sweet smile	Tens um sorriso lindo *taynz oom sooreesoo leendoo*
You have such beautiful eyes	Tens uns olhos tão lindos *taynz oonz ollyoosh tau leendoosh*
I'm in love with you	Estou apaixonado/a por ti *eshtoe appaishonardoo/a por tee*
I'm in love with you too	E eu por ti *ee ew por tee*
I love you	Amo-te *ammoo tuh*
I love you too	Eu também te amo *ew taubaim tee ammoo*
I don't feel as strongly about you	Não sinto um grande amor por ti *now oo seentoo oom grand amor por tee*
I already have a boyfriend/girlfriend	Já tenho um namorado/uma namorada *jah tenyoo oom namorardoo/ooma namorardah*
I'm not ready for that	Ainda não cheguei a esse ponto *ayeenda now shegay ah ess pontoo*
This is going too fast for me	Eu preciso de mais tempo *ew preseezoo duh mysh tempoo*
Take your hands off me	Não te metas comigo *nao tuh metash commeegoo*
Okay, no problem	Está bem, não faz mal *estah baim now faj mal*
Will you stay with me tonight?	Ficas esta noite comigo? *feecash eshtah noyt commeegoo?*
I'd like to go to bed with you	Quero ir para a cama contigo *keroo eer parra ah camma conteegoo*
Only if we use a condom	Só com um preservativo *soh com oom preservateevoo*
We have to be careful about AIDS	Temos de ser cautelosos com a SIDA *taymoosh de sair cowtellozush com ah seeda*
That's what they all say	É o que todos dizem *eh oo kuh toedoosh deezaim*
We shouldn't take any risks	Não podemos correr riscos *now poodaymoosh correr reeshcush*
Do you have a condom?	Tens um preservativo? *taynz oom preservateevoo?*
No? In that case we won't do it	Não? Então não podemos *now? entau now poodaymoosh*

3.11 Arrangements

When will I see you again?	Quando é que te volto a ver?/Quando é que vejo você de novo? *cwarndoo eh kuh tuh voltoo ah vair?*
Are you free over the weekend?	Tem tempo no fim-de-semana? *taim tempoo noo feem duh semarna?*
What shall we arrange?	O que é que combinamos? *oo ki eh kuh combinarmoosh?*
Where shall we meet?	Onde nos encontramos? *one nuz encontrarmoosh?*
Will you pick me/us up?	Vem buscar-me/nos? *vaim booshcar muh/noosh?*
Shall I pick you up?	Posso ir buscálo/la? *possoo eer bushcar loo/la?*
I have to be home by...	Tenho de estar em casa às... *tenyoo di eshtar aim carza aj...*
I don't want to see you anymore	Não o/a quero ver mais *now oo/ah kairoo vair mysh*

3.12 Saying goodbye

Can I take you home?	Posso levá-lo/la para casa? *possoo levar loo/la parra carza?*
Can I write/call you?	Posso escrever-lhe/telefonar-lhe? *possoo eshcrevair lya/teleffonar lya?*
Will you write/call me?	Escreve me/telefóna-me? *eshcrev muh/teleffona muh?*
Can I have your address/phone number?	Dá me a sua morada/o seu telefone? *dar muh ah sua morrarda/oo sayoo telefon?*
Thanks for everything	Obrigado por tudo *obrigardoo por toodoo*
It was very nice	Gostei imenso *goshtay immensoo*
Say hello to...	Cumprimentos a... *coomprimentoosh ah...*
All the best	Desejo-te o melhor *dezayjoo tuh oo mellyor*
Good luck	Que tudo corra bem *kuh toodoo corrah baim*
When will you be back?	Quando voltas? *cwarndoo volltash*
I'll be waiting for you	Espero por ti *eshpairoo por tee*
I'd like to see you again	Gostava de voltar a ver-te *goshtarva duh volltar ah vair tuh*
I hope we meet again soon	Espero que a gente volte a se ver brevemente *eshpairoo kuh ah jent vollt ah suh vair brevment*
This is our address. If you're ever in the UK...	Esta é a nossa morada. Se algum dia for à Inglaterra... *eshta eh ah nossa morardah. se algoom deeah for ah eenglaterrah...*
You'd be more than welcome	É sempre bem-vindo *eh semprah baim veendoo*

4

Eating out

4 Eating out

● **In Portugal** people usually have at least three meals:
Breakfast (*pequeno almoço*) is taken between 7.30 and 10 am. Breakfast is light and consists of *café com leite* (white coffee) and rolls and butter (*pão com manteiga*) or toast (*torradas*).
Lunch (*almoço*) is taken between midday and 2pm. It is usually quite a substantial meal and is never rushed. Offices and shops often close and lunch is taken at home or in a restaurant or café. The meal usually consists of at least two courses and is often preceded by soup. Bread is usually available on the table.
Dinner (*jantar*) is from 8pm onwards and is similar in content to lunch. It is usually a family meal taken at home, except at weekends and public holidays when restaurants are the preferred venue.
Some Portuguese manage to fit in *lanche* (tea) during the afternoon whilst most cannot last until the evening meal without a snack of some sort. Late night supper (*ceia*) is available in some bars and small restaurants around midnight.

4.1 On arrival

I'd like to book a table for seven o'clock, please	Posso reservar uma mesa para as sete? *possoo resairvar ooma mayza parra ash set?*
I'd like a table for two, please	Uma mesa para duas pessoas, se faz favor *ooma mayza parra dooash pessoash, suh faj favvor*
We've/we haven't booked	(Não) reservámos *(now) resairvarmoosh*
Is the restaurant open yet?	O restaurante já está aberto? *oo reshtowrant jah eshtah abertoo?*
What time does the restaurant open/close?	A que horas abre/fecha o restaurante? *ah kay orash abre/fesha oo reshtowrant?*
Can we wait for a table?	Podemos esperar por uma mesa? *poddaymoosh eshpairar por ooma mayza?*
Will we have to wait long?	Temos de esperar muito tempo? *taymoosh di eshpairar mweentoo tempoo?*
Is this seat taken?	Este lugar está livre? *esht loogar eshtah leevre*
Can we sit here/there?	Podemos sentar aqui/alí? *poodaymoosh sentar akee/alee?*
Can we sit by the window?	Podemos sentar junto à janela? *podaymoosh sentar joontoo ah janella?*
Can we eat outside?	Também podemos comer lá fora? *taubaim poodaymoosh comair la foura?*

Reservou uma mesa?	Do you have a reservation?
Em que nome?	What name, please?
Por aqui, se faz favor	This way, please
Esta mesa está reservada	This table is reserved
Dentro de uns quinze minutos uma mesa fica livre	We'll have a table free in fifteen minutes
Entretanto, importava-se de esperar (no bar)?	Would you like to wait (at the bar)?

Do you have another chair for us?	Pode-nos trazer mais uma cadeira?	*pod noosh trazair maiz uma cadairah?*
Do you have a highchair?	Pode-nos trazer uma cadeira de criança?	*pod noosh trazer ooma cadaira de criansa?*
Is there a socket for this bottle-warmer?	Há uma tomada para se ligar este aquecedor de biberão?	*hah ooma toomarda parra suh ligar esht akessedor duh beeberow?*
Could you warm up this bottle/jar for me?	Poderia aquecer esta garrafa/este boião?	*pooderia akessair eshta garraffa/este boyau?*
Not too hot, please	Não muito quente, se faz favor	*now mweentoo kent, suh faj favvor*
Is there somewhere I can change the baby's nappy?	Há aqui algum lugar onde eu possa arranjar o bébé?	*hah akee algoom loogar ond eu possa arranjar oo behbeh?*
Where are the toilets?	Onde são os lavabos?	*ond sow oosh lavarboosh?*

4.2 Ordering

Waiter!	Senhor empregado!/Garçon!	*senyor empregardoo!/garsonn!*
Madam!	Minha senhora!	*meenya senyora!*
Sir!	Senhor!	*senyor!*
We'd like something to eat/a drink	Nós gostaríamos de comer/beber alguma coisa	*noj goshtariamosh duh commair/bebbair algooma coyza*
Could I have a quick meal?	Poderia comer alguma coisa rapidamente?	*pooderia commair algooma coyza rappeedament?*
We don't have much time	Temos pouco tempo	*taymoosh poecoo tempoo*
We'd like to have a drink first	Primeiro queríamos beber qualquer coisa	*preemayroo kerriamoosh bebbair qualcair coyza*
Could we see the menu/wine list, please?	Poderia dar nos a ementa/lista de vinhos?	*pooderia dar noosh ah ementa/leeshta duh veenyoosh?*
Do you have a menu in English?	Tem uma ementa em inglês?	*taim ooma ementa aim inglayj?*
Do you have a dish of the day?	Tem um prato do dia/menu turístico?	*taim oom prarto do dia/menu tureeshteeco?*
We haven't made a choice yet	Ainda não escolhemos	*eyeenda now eshcolyemoosh*
What do you recommend?	O que é que nos recomenda?	*oo kee eh kuh noosh recomenda*
What are the specialities of the region/the house?	Quais são as especialidades da região/da casa?	*quysh sow az eshpecialidardesh duh regiau/duh carza?*
I like strawberries/olives	Gosto de morangos/de azeitonas	*goshtoo duh morangoosh/de azaytonnash*

Eating out

I don't like fish/meat...	Não gosto de peixe/de carne *now goshtoo duh paysh/duh carn/duh...*
What's this?	O que é isto? *oo ki eh ishtoo*
Does it have...in it?	Isto leva...? *ishtoo levva?*
What does it look like/ taste like?	Com o que é que se parece?/Tem gosto de quê? *com oo ki eh kuh suh paress?/taim gostoo duh kay?*
Is it a hot or a cold dish?	É um prato frio ou quente? *eh oom prartoo freeoo o kent?*
Is it sweet?	É um prato doce? *eh oom prartoo dose?*
Is it spicy?	É um prato picante/com muitos temperos? *eh oom prartoo picant/com mweentoosh temperoosh?*
Do you have anything else, please?	Tem por acaso outra coisa? *taim por acarzoo ohtra coyza?*
I'm on a salt-free diet	Não posso comer sal *now possoo commair sal*
I can't eat pork	Não posso comer carne de porco *now possoo commair carn duh porcoo*
– sugar	Não posso comer açúcar *now possoo commair assoocar*
– fatty foods	Não posso comer gorduras *now possoo commair gordourash*
– (hot) spices	Não posso comer coisas muito picantes *now possoo commair coyzash mweentoo picantesh*
I'll/we'll have what those people are having	O mesmo que aqueles senhores, se faz favor *oo mejmoo kuh akelesh senyoresh suh faj favvor*
I'd like...	Para mim... *parra me...*
We're not having a starter	Não queremos entrada *now keraymoosh entrarda*
The child will share what we're having	O menino come alguma coisa do nosso prato *oo meneenoo com algooma coyza doo nossoo prartoo*

Desejam tomar uma bebida primeiro?	Would you like a drink first?
Já escolheram?	Have you decided?
O que querem beber?	What would you like to drink?
Bom proveito	Enjoy your meal
Querem uma sobremesa/ tomar café?	Would you like a dessert/coffee?
Eu queria ainda uma aguardente, se faz favor	I'd like a brandy please

Eating out 4

Could I have some more bread, please?	Traga nos mais pão, se faz favor *tragga noosh mysh pow, suh faj favvor*
– a bottle of water/wine	Traga nos uma garrafa de água/de vinho, se faz favor *tragga nooz ooma garraffa duh agwa/duh veenyoo, suh faj favvor*
– another helping of...	Traga nos mais uma dose de..., se faz favor *tragga nooj myz ooma doz duh ..., suh faj favvor*
– some salt and pepper	Poderia trazer sal e pimenta, se faz favor? *pooderia trazair sal ee peementa suh faj favvor?*
– a napkin	Poderia trazer um guardanapo? *pooderia trazair oom gwardanarpoo?*
– a spoon	Poderia trazer uma colher? *pooderia trazair ooma coolyer?*
– an ashtray	Poderia trazer um cinzeiro? *pooderia trazair oom seenzayroo?*
– some matches	Poderia trazer fósforos? *pooderia trazair foshferoosh?*
– some toothpicks	Poderia trazer palitos? *pooderia trazair paleetoosh?*
– a glass of water	Poderia trazer um copo de água? *pooderia trazair oom coppoo d'agwa?*
– a straw (for the child)	Poderia trazer uma palhinha (para o menino)? *pooderia trazair ooma pallyeenya (parra o meneeno)?*
Enjoy your meal!	Bom proveito! *bom proovaytoo*
You too!	Igualmente! *eegwalmente*
Cheers!	À sua saúde! *ah sooah sowood*
The next round's on me	A próxima rodada eu pago *ah prossima roodarda ew pargoo*
Could we have a doggy bag, please?	Podemos levar o resto para o nosso cão? *podaymoosh levvar oo reshtoo parra oo nossoo cow?*
How much is this dish?	Qual é o preço deste prato? *cuarl eh oo praysoo desht partoo?*

4.3 The bill

See also 8.2 Settling the bill

Could I have the bill, please?	A conta, se faz favor *ah conta suh faj favvor*
All together	Tudo junto *toodoo joontoo*
Everyone pays separately	Cada um paga a sua parte *carda oom parga ah sooah part*
Could we have the menu again, please?	Podemos ver a ementa novamente? *podaymoosh vair ah ementa novvament?*
The...is not on the bill	O/A...não está na conta *ah/oo...now eshtah nah conta*

4.4 Complaints

It's taking a very long time	Está a demorar muito tempo *eshtah ah demorar mweentoo tempoo*
We've been here an hour already	Já aqui estamos há uma hora *jah akee eshtamoosh ah ooma ora*
This must be a mistake	Isto deve ser engano *ishtoo dev sair engarnoo*
This is not what I ordered	Isto não é o que pedi *ishtoo now eh oo que peddee*
I ordered...	Pedi um/uma ... *peddee oom/ooma...*
There's a dish missing	Falta um prato *falta oom prartoo*
This is broken/not clean	Isto está partido/sujo *ishtoo eshtah parteedoo/soojoo*
The food's cold	A comida está fria *ah comeeda eshtah freea*
– not fresh	A comida não é fresca *ah comeeda now eh freshca*
– too salty/sweet/spicy	A comida está salgada/doce/ condimentada *ah comeeda eshtah salgarda/doess/ condimentarda*
The meat's not done	A carne está crua *ah carn eshtah crooa*
– overdone	A carne está cozida demais *a carn eshtah coozeeda demysh*
– tough	A carne está dura *a carn eh reeja*
– off	A carne está estragada *a carn eshtah shtragarda*
Could I have something else instead of this?	Podia trazer me outra coisa em vez disto? *poodia trazair muh ohtra coyza aim vej deeshtoo?*
The bill/this amount is not right	A conta/o total não está certa(o) *ah conta/oo tootal now eshtah sairta(oo)*
We didn't have this	Isto não nos foi servido *eeshtoo now nooj foi serveedoo*
There's no paper in the toilet	Não há papel higiénico na casa de banho *now ah papell hijenneecoo nah carza duh bahnyoo*
Do you have a complaints book?	Tem um livro de reclamações? *taim oom leevroo duh reclammasoynsh?*
Will you call the manager, please?	Podia chamar o gerente, se faz favor? *poodia shammar oo jerent, suh faj favvor?*

4.5 Paying a compliment

That was a wonderful meal	Comemos muito bem *comaymoosh mweentoo baim*
The food was excellent	A comida estava excelente *ah comeeda eshtarva eshsellent*
The...in particular was delicious	Principalmente o/a...estava excelente *preencipallment oo/ah...eshtarva eshcellent*

4.6 The menu

aperitivos
appetisers
aves
poultry
bebidas alcoólicas
alcoholic beverages
bebidas quentes
hot beverages
caça
game
cocktails
cocktails
entradas (quentes/frias)
hot/cold starters
especialidades (regionais)
(regional) specialities
legumes
vegetables
lista dos vinhos
the wine list
marisco
shellfish
pastelaria/doces
confectionery/desserts
salgados
savouries
prato do dia
dish of the day
prato principal
main course
pratos de carne
meat courses
pratos frios
cold dishes
pratos quentes
hot dishes
queijo
cheese
refrescos
cold drinks
serviço incluído
service included
sobremesas
sweets
sopas
soups

4.7 Alphabetical list of drinks and dishes

açorda/camaróes à milanesa com alho
prawns with garlic and breadcrumbs
açúcar
sugar
agua mineral sem/com gás
sparkling/still mineral water
aguardente
brandy
alcachofra
artichoke
alcaparras
capers
alface
lettuce
alho
garlic
alho francês
leek
almôndegas
meatballs
amêijoas
clams
ameixas
plums
ameixas secas
prunes
amêndoas
almonds
ananás
pineapple
anchova
anchovy
aniz
aniseed
aperitivos
aperitives
arroz
rice
assado
roast
atum
tuna
avelã
hazelnut
azeitonas
olives
bacalhão
cod (dried)
banana
banana
batatas fritas
chips
batatas
potatoes
batido de...
...milkshake
bebidas alcoólicas
alcoholic beverages
bebidas frescas/quentes
cool/hot drinks
beringela
aubergine
bica
coffee - expresso
bife
steak
bife do lombo
sirloin steak
bolachas
biscuits
bolo
bun
bolo de chocolate
chocolate bun
cabrito
kid
café (com leite)
coffee (white)
caldeirada
stew
camarões grandes
prawns
camarões
shrimps

canja
broth
caracóis
snails
caranguejo
crab
carioca
coffee - weak, without milk
carne
meat
carne de porco
pork
carne picada
ground beef
castanhas
chestnuts
cebola
onion
cebolinha
shallot
cenouras
carrots
cerejas
cherries
cerveja
beer
chá
tea
chantilly
cream (whipped)
chouriço
smoked preserved sausage
cocktails
cocktails
codorniz
quail
coelho
rabbit
cogumelos
mushrooms
costeleta
cutlet
costeleta de porco
pork chop
couve
cabbage
couve-flor
cauliflower
cozido
stew
cravinho
clove
crepes
crepes
croquetes (de carne)
croquettes (meat)
cru
raw
talheres
cutlery
dobrada
tripe
doce
sweet
entradas
starters
ervas
herbs
ervilhas
peas
espargos
asparagus
esparguete
spaghetti
especialidades da região
regional specialities
especiarias
spices
espinafre
spinach
farinha
flour
favas
broad beans
feijão branco/ encarnado/frade/ verde
beans: haricot/ kidney/ green
fiambre
ham
fígado
liver
figo
fig
filé
fillet steak
filete
fillet
filé de vitela
fillet of veal
framboesas
raspberries
frango
chicken
frango no churrasco
barbecued chicken
frito
fried
fruta (da época)
fruit (of the season)
frutos do mar
seafood
fumado
smoked
galão
coffee - large white
gaspacho
chilled soup (tomato and cucumber)
gelado
ice cream
gelo
ice
grão
chick pea
grelhado
grilled
groselhas
red currents
guisado
stew
imperial
draught beer
iogurte
yogurt
língua-de-vaca
tongue
lagosta
lobster
lagostim
crayfish
laranjas
oranges
legumes
vegetables
leite gordo/meio magro/magro
milk - full cream/ semi skimmed/ skimmed
lentilhas
lentils
licor
liqueur
limão
lemon
limonada
lemonade

linguado
sole
lista de vinho
wine list
lombo de porco
loin of pork
lombo de vaca
sirloin steak
lulas
squid
maçã
apple
mal passado (bife)
rare (beef)
manteiga
butter
maracujá
passion fruit
margarina
margerine
mariscos
shellfish
marmelada
jam
melão
melon
mexilhões
mussels
milho
sweetcorn
miolos
sweetbreads
morangos
strawberries
morcela
black pudding
mostarda
mustard
mousse de chocolate
chocolate mousse
nata
cream
nozes
nuts
omeleta
omelette
ostras
oysters
ovo quente/cozido/ estrelado/escalofad o/ mexido
egg - soft/hard/fried/ poached/scrambled
pão
bread
pãozinho
roll
pêra
pear
pêssego
peach
paio
smoked sausage
panqueque
pancake
pargo
sea bream
passas
raisins
pastel de nata
small custard tart
pastelaria
pastry
pato
duck
peito
breast
peixe
fish
peixe frito (carapau)
small fried fish similar to whitebait
peixe espada
sword-fish
pepino
cucumber
perdiz
partridge
perna de borrego
leg of lamb
perú
turkey
pescada
whiting
pimenta
pepper (condiment)
pimento
green/red pepper
pizza
pizza
polvo
octopus
prato do dia
dish of the day
prato frio/quente
cold/hot course
prato principal
main course
presunto
parma ham
pudim
pudding
pudim flan
creme caramel
queijo
cheese
rabanete
radish
recheado
filled, stuffed
rissol
rissole
robalo
sea bass
rodovalho
turbot
rosbife
roast beef
sal
salt
salada
salad
salada russa
salad with mayonnaise
salgadinhos
savoury snacks
salgado/doce
savoury/sweet
salmão
salmon
salmão fumado
smoked salmon
salmonete
red mullet
salsa
parsley
sandes
sandwich
sardinhas
sardines
seco
dry
serviço (não) incluído
service (not) included
sobremesa
dessert
sopa
soup
sopa de cebola
onion soup
sopa de feijão
bean soup
sumo de fruta
fruit juice

sumo de laranja
orange juice
sumo de limão
lemon juice
tâmara
fig
tamboril
monk fish
tarte de maçã
apple tart
tomate
tomato
tomilho
thyme
torrada
toast
tosta mista
toasted cheese and ham sandwich
toucinho
bacon
truta
trout
truta salmoneja
salmon trout
uvas
grapes
vitela
veal
veado
venison
vinagre
vinegar
vinho branco
white wine
vinho rosé
rosé wine
vinho tinto
red wine
xerez
sherry

5

On the road

5 On the road

5.1 Asking for directions

Excuse me, could I ask you something?	Desculpe, posso-lhe fazer uma pergunta? *deshcoolp possoo lher fazair ooma pergoonta?*
I've lost my way	Perdi-me *perdee muh*
Is there a... around here?	Conhece um...perto daqui? *coonyes oom...pairtoo dakee?*
Is this the way to...?	É este o caminho para...? *eh esht oo cameenyoo parra...?*
Could you tell me how to get to the... (name of place) by car/on foot?	Poderia dizer-me como devo fazer para ir para...a pé/de carro? *pooderia dizair muh como dayvoo fazair parra eer parra...ah peh/duh cahroo?*
What's the quickest way to...?	Como é que chego o mais depressa possível a...? *como eh kuh chaygoo oo mysh depressa posseevel ah...?*
How many kilometres is it to...?	Quantos quilómetros faltam ainda para chegar a...? *cuarntoosh keelometroosh faltam ayeenda parra sheggar ah...?*
Could you point it out on the map?	Poderia indicar-me aqui no mapa? *pooderiah eendiccar muh akee noo mappa?*

Não sei, não conheço isto aqui	I don't know, I don't know my way around here
Está enganado	You're going the wrong way
Tem de voltar a...	You have to go back to...
Aí as placas indicam-lhe o caminho a seguir	From there on just follow the signs
Aí deve perguntar de novo	When you get there, ask again

em frente straight ahead	cruzamento intersection	passagem de nível; cancelas level crossing
à esquerda left	estrada street	placa indicando o caminho à... sign pointing to...
à direita right	semáforo traffic light	ponte bridge
cortar turn	placa de trânsito \`cruzamento com prioridade' \`give way' sign	seta arrow
seguir follow	rio river	
atravessar cross		

5.2 Customs

● **Documents**: valid passport, visa. For car and motorbike: valid UK driving licence and registration document, insurance document, green card, UK registration plate. Caravan: must be entered on the green card and be driven with the same registration number. An inventory in either Portuguese, English or French of its contents must be available (this also applies to trailers) to show customs. A warning triangle, headlamp converters and extra headlamp bulbs must be carried. Insurance should also be upgraded.
Import and export specifications:
– Foreign currency: no restrictions
– Alcohol (if aged 17 and above): 10 litres of spirits and 90 litres of wine. Tobacco (if aged 17 and above): 800 cigarettes, 200 cigars or a kilo of tobacco. Restricted to personal consumption only.

O seu passaporte, se faz favor	Your passport, please
A carta verde, se faz favor	Your green card, please
O livrete, se faz favor	Your vehicle documents, please
O seu visto, se faz favor	Your visa, please
Para onde vai?	Where are you heading?
Quanto tempo pensa ficar?	How long are you planning to stay?
Tem alguma coisa a declarar?	Do you have anything to declare?
Pode abrir isto?	Open this, please

My children are entered on this passport	Os meus filhos estão inscritos neste passaporte *oosh mayoosh feelyoosh eshtau eenshcreetoosh nest passaport*
I'm travelling through	Estou de passagem *eshtoe duh passarjaim*
I'm going on holiday to...	Vou de férias para... *voe duh ferriash parra...*
I'm on a business trip	Estou em viagem de negócios *eshtoe aim veearjaim duh neggossioosh*
I don't know how long I'll be staying yet	Ainda não sei quanto tempo fico *ayeenda now say cuarntoo tempoo feecoo*
I'll be staying here for a weekend	Fico aqui um fim-de-semana *feecoo akee oom feem duh semarna*
– for a few days	Fico aqui uns dias *feecoo akee unsh deeash*
– for a week	Fico aqui uma semana *feecoo akee ooma semarna*
– for two weeks	Fico aqui duas semanas *feecoo akee dooash semarnash*
I've got nothing to declare	Não tenho nada a declarar *now tenyoo narda a declarar*
I've got...with me	Trago comigo... *trargoo comeegoo...*

– ...cartons of cigarettes	Trago comigo um pacote de cigarros *trargoo comeegoo oom pacott de sigaroosh*
– ...bottles of...	Trago comigo uma garrafa de... *trargoo comeegoo ooma garrafa duh...*
– some souvenirs	Trago comigo algumas lembranças *trargoo comeegoo algoomash lembransash*
These are personal effects	Estas são coisas pessoais *eshtash sow coyzash pessooaish*
These are not new	Estas coisas não são novas *eshtash coyzash now sow novash*
Here's the receipt	Aqui está o recibo *akee eshtah oo receeboo*
This is for private use	Isto é para uso pessoal *eeshtoo eh parra oozoo pessooarl*
How much import duty do I have to pay?	Quanto tenho de pagar de direitos? *cuarntoo tenyoo duh pagar duh diraytoosh?*
Can I go now?	Posso ir agora? *possoo eer agoora?*

5.3 Luggage

Porter!	Bagageiro!/Carregador! *bagajayroo!/carreggadoor!*
Could you take this luggage to...?	Podia levar esta bagagem para..., se faz favor? *poodia levvar eshtah bagarjaim parra..., suh faj favvor?*
How much do I owe you?	Quanto lhe devo? *cuarntoo lyer dayvoo?*
Where can I find a luggage trolley?	Onde estão os carrinhos para a bagagem? *onde eshtau oosh careenyoosh parra ah bagarjaim?*
Could you store this luggage for me?	Posso colocor esta bagagem no depósito? *possoo coloocar eshta bagarjaim noo deposittoo?*
Where are the luggage lockers?	Onde estão os cofres para bagagem? *ond eshtau oosh coffresh parra bagarjaim?*
I can't get the locker open	Não consigo abrir este cofre *nau conseegoo abreer esht coffre*
How much is it per item per day?	Quanto custa um volume por dia? *cuarntoo cooshta oom voloom por deah?*
This is not my bag/ suitcase	Isto não é o meu saco/a minha mala *eeshtoo now eh oo mayoo sarcoo/ah meenya mala*
There's one item/bag/ suitcase missing still	Ainda falta um volume/um saco/uma mala *ayeenda falta oom voloom/oom sarcoo/ooma mala*
My suitcase is damaged	A minha mala está danificada *ah meenya mala eshtah daneefeecarda*

5.4 Traffic signs

aberto
open
animais cruzando
animals crossing
auto-estrada (com portagem)
motorway (with tolls)
bermas baixas
low hard-shoulder
bifurcação
road fork
centro da cidade
city centre
circule pela direita
keep right
circule pela esquerda
keep left
cruzamento perigoso
dangerous crossroads
cuidado
caution
curva a...quilómetros
road bends in... kilometres
curva perigosa
dangerous bend
dê passegem
give way
desvio
diversion
devagar
slow down
espere
wait
estacionamento
parking
estacionamento proibido
no parking
estrada em mau estado
irregular road surface
estrada interrompida
no through road
estrada nacional
main road
excepto
except
fechado
closed
fim de...
end of...
fim de obras
end of roadworks
gelo
ice on road
neve
snow
nevoeiro
fog
obras
road works
passagem de nivel (sem guarda)
level crossing (unmanned)
perigo
danger
portagem
toll
posto de primeiros socorros
First Aid Post
saída
exit
sentido único
one-way street
vedado ao trânsito
road closed
veículos pesados
heavy vehicles
velocidade máxima
maximum speed
via de acesso
access only

5.5 The car

See the diagram on page 49.

● **Particular traffic regulations:**
– maximum speed for cars:
120km/h on motorways
90km/h outside built-up areas
60km/h in built-up areas
– give way: traffic on the main road has priority but at intersections of equal priority traffic from the right has priority

5.6 The petrol station

● **Petrol is** more expensive in Portugal than in many other countries. Portugal has a good network of motorway service stations and filling stations, most of which accept payment by credit card.

How many kilometres to the next petrol station, please?
Quantos quilómetros faltam para a próxima bomba de gasolina?
cuarntoosh keelometroosh faltam parra ah prossima bomba de gasooleena?

I would like...litres of...,	Quero...litros de... *kairoo...leetroosh duh...*
– super petrol	Quero...litros de gasolina super *kairoo...leeroosh duh gazooleena super*
– leaded petrol	Quero...litros de gasolina normal *kairoo...leetroosh duh gazooleena normal*
– unleaded petrol	Quero...litros de gasolina sem chumbo *kairoo...leetroosh duh gazoleena saim shoomboo*
– diesel	Quero...litros de gasóleo *kairoo...leetroosh duh gazollio*
I would like...escudos' worth of..., please	Quero...escudos de..., se faz favor *kairoo...eshcoodoosh duh..., suh faj favvor*
Fill her up, please	Encha se faz favor *ensha suh faj favvor*
Could you check...?	Não se importava de ver...? *now se importarva duh vair...?*
– the oil level	Não se importava de ver o nível do óleo? *now se importarva duh vair oo neevel doo ollio?*
– the tyre pressure	Não se importava de ver a pressão dos pneus? *now se importarva duh vair ah pressow doosh penayoosh?*
Could you change the oil, please?	Podia mudar o óleo? *poodia moodar oo ollio?*
Could you clean the windows/the windscreen, please?	Podia limpar os vidros/o pára-brisas? *poodia leempar oosh vidroosh/oo parra-breezash?*
Could you give the car a wash, please?	Podia dar uma lavagem ao carro? *poodia dar ooma lavarjaim ow cahroo?*

5.7 Breakdown and repairs

I'm having car trouble. Could you give me a hand?	Tenho uma avaria. Poderia ajudar-me? *tenyoo ooma avveriah. pooderia ajoodar-muh?*
I've run out of petrol	Estou sem gasolina *eshtoe saim gazoleena*
I've locked the keys in the car	Deixei as chaves dentro do carro *dayshay ash sharvesh dentroo doo cahroo*
The car/motorbike/ moped won't start	O carro/a mota/a motorizada não arranca *oo cahroo/ah motta/ah motoreezarda now aranca*
Could you contact the rescue service for me, please?	Poderia avisar o pronto socorro da ACP? *pooderia aveezar oo prontoo socoroo da ey say pay?*
Could you call a garage for me, please?	Poderia telefonar para uma oficina? *pooderia telefonar parra ooma offeeseena?*

The parts of a car

(the diagram shows the numbered parts)

1	battery	bateria	*batteria*
2	rear light	luz da retaguarda	*looj da rettagwarda*
3	rear-view mirror	espelho retrovisor	*eshpelyoo retrooveesor*
	reversing light	farol de marcha atrás	*farol duh marcha atraj*
4	aerial	antena	*antenna*
	car radio	rádio	*rahdioo*
5	petrol tank	depósito de gasolina	*depozitoo duh gazooleena*
6	sparking plugs	velas	*vellash*
	fuel filter/pump	filtro/bomba de gasolina	*feeltroo/bomba duh gazooleena*
7	wing mirror	espelho exterior	*eshpelyoo eshterrior*
8	bumper	pára-choques	*para shocksh*
	carburettor	carburador	*carbooradoor*
	crankcase	cárter	*cartair*
	cylinder	cilindro	*seeleendroo*
	ignition	platinados	*platteenardoosh*
	warning light	luz de controle	*l ooj duh controal*
	dynamo	dínamo	*deenamoo*
	accelerator	acelerador	*asselleradoor*
	handbrake	travão de mão	*travow duh mau*
	valve	válvula	*vallvoola*
9	silencer	silenciador	*seelenciadoor*
10	boot	mala	*marla*
11	headlight	farol da frente	*faroll da frent*
	crank shaft	eixo da manivela	*ayshoo da manivela*
12	air filter	filtro do ar	*feeltroo doo ar*
	fog lamp	faróis de nevoeiro	*faroysh duh nevooayroo*
13	engine block	motor	*mottor*
	camshaft	árvore de cames	*arvora duh camesh*
	oil filter/pump	filtro/bomba do óleo	*feeltroo/bomba doo ollio*
	dipstick	vareta	*varetta*
	pedal	pedal	*pedarl*
14	door	porta	*porta*
15	radiator	radiador	*raddiadoor*
16	brake disc	disco do travão	*deeshcoo doo travow*
	spare wheel	roda sobresselente	*rodda sobresallent*
17	indicator	pisca-pisca	*peeshca-peeshca*
18	windscreen wiper	limpa pára-brisas	*leempa parra-breezash*
19	shock absorbers	pára-choques	*parra shocksh*
	sunroof	janela do tejadilho	*janella doo taijadeelhoo*
	spoiler	spoiler	*spoiler*
	starter motor	motor de arranque	*motor di arrank*
20	steering column	caixa de direccão	*caisha duh deeresow*
21	exhaust pipe	tubo de escape	*tooboo duh eshcape*
22	seat belt	cinto de segurança	*seentoo duh seguransa*
	fan	ventoinha	*ventooeenya*
23	distributor cables	cabos conductores	*carboosh condootoresh*

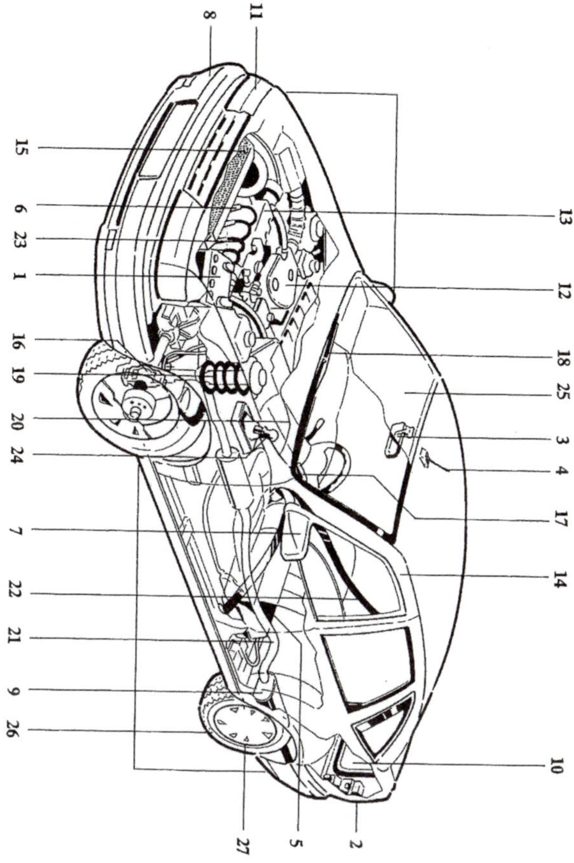

24 gear lever	alavanca das mudanças	*alavanca dash moodansash*
25 windscreen	pára-brisas	*parra breezash*
water pump	bomba de água	*bomba de agwa*
26 wheel	roda	*rodda*
27 hubcap	tampo de roda	*tampoo duh rodda*
piston	êmbolo	*aimboloo*

Could you give me a lift to...? — Posso ir consigo até a...?
possoo eer conseegoo atay ah...?

– a garage/into town? — Posso ir consigo até a uma oficina/à cidade?
possoo eer conseegoo atay ooma offiseena/ah sidarda?

– a phone booth? — Posso ir consigo até a uma cabine telefónica?
Possoo eer conseegoo atay ooma cabeen telefonica?

– an emergency phone? — Posso ir consigo até a um telefone de urgência?
possoo eer conseegoo atay ah oom telefon duh urgencia?

Can we take my bicycle/moped? — Posso levar também a minha bicicleta/motorizada?
possoo levar tambaim ah meenya beeceecleta/motoreezarda?

Could you tow me to a garage? — Poderia rebocar-me até a uma garagem?
pooderia reboocar-muh atay ooma gararjaim?

There's probably something wrong with... (See page 48) — Creio que há algum problema com...
crayoo kuh ha algoom proobllema com...

Can you fix it? — Poderia consertar isso?
pooderia consertar eesoo?

Could you fix my tyre? — Poderia consertar-me o pneu?
pooderia consertar-muh oo punayoo?

Could you change this wheel? — Poderia mudar esta roda?
pooderia moodar eshta rodda?

Can you fix it so it'll get me to...? — Poderia arranjar isto de maneira que possa seguir até...
pooderia arranjar eeshtoo duh manayra kuh possoo segear atay...

Which garage can help me? — Que oficina poderá me ajudar?
kay offiseena poodera muh ajoodar?

When will my car/bicycle be ready? — Quando o meu carro/a minha bicicleta fica pronto/pronta?
cuarndoo oo mayoo cahroo/ah meenya beeseeclaytah feeca prontoo/pronta?

Can I wait for it here? — Posso esperar aqui?
possoo eshpairar akee?

How much will it cost? — Quanto é que vai custar?
cuarntoo eh kuh vy cooshtar?

Could you itemise the bill? — Poderia especificar a factura?
pooderia eshpeceefeecar ah fatoora?

Can I have a receipt for the insurance? — Pode dar-me um recibo para a companhia de seguros?
pod dar muh oom receeboo parra ah companyeea duh segooroosh?

Não tenho peças para o seu carro/a sua bicicleta	I don't have parts for your car/bicycle
Tenho de ir buscar as peças em outro lugar	I have to get the parts from somewhere else
Tenho de encomendar as peças	I have to order the parts
Isto leva meio-dia	That'll take half a day
Isto dura um dia	That'll take a day
Isto dura uns dias	That'll take a few days
Isto dura uma semana	That'll take a week
O seu carro vai para a sucata	Your car is a write-off
Já não há nada a fazer	It can't be repaired.
O carro/a mota/a motorizada está pronto/pronta às...horas	The car/motor bike/moped/bicycle will be ready at... o'clock.

5.8 The bicycle/moped

See the diagram on page 53.

● **Cycling/riding mopeds** on the roads can be dangerous in Portugal as riders are largely disregarded by motorists, but there are some interesting off-road tracks (unmarked). Rented cycles are few and far between so it is advisable for visitors to bring their own – and a crash helmet.

5.9 Renting a vehicle

I'd like to rent a...	Eu gostaria de alugar um... *eyoo goshtaria duh aloogar oom...*
Do I need a (special) licence for that?	Preciso de ter uma carta de condução especial? *preseezoo duh tair ooma carta duh condoosow eshpessial?*
I'd like to rent the...for...	Gostaria de alugar o...por... *gostaria duh aloogar oo...por...*
– one day	Gostaria de alugar o...por um dia *gostaria duh aloogar oo...por oom deeah*
– two days	Gostaria de alugar o...por dois dias *gostaria duh aloogar oo...por doysh deeash*
How much is that per day/week?	Quanto custa por dia/por semana? *cuarntoo cooshta por deeah/por semarna?*
How much is the deposit?	Quanto é o depósito? *cuarntoo eh oo depozeetoo?*
Could I have a receipt for the deposit?	Pode dar-me um recibo do depósito? *pod dar muh oom resseeboo doo depozeetoo?*
How much is the surcharge per kilometre?	Quanto tenho a pagar por cada quilómetro extra? *cuarntoo tenyoo ah paggar por carda keelometroo estra?*
Does that include petrol?	A gasolina está incluída? *ah gazooleena eshtah eenclooeeda?*
Does that include insurance?	O seguro está incluído? *oo segooroo eshtah eenclooeedoo?*

The parts of a bicycle

(the diagram shows the numbered parts)

1	rear lamp	luz da retaguarda	*ooj da retagwarda*
2	rear wheel	pneu de trás	*penayoo duh traj*
3	(luggage) carrier	porta bagagem	*porta bagarjaim*
4	bicycle fork	caixa de esferas	*caysha di eshfairash*
5	bell	campainha	*campyeenya*
	inner tube	câmara de ar	*camera di ar*
	tyre	pneu	*penayoo*
6	crank	crenque	*crenk*
7	gear change	alavanca das velocidades	*alavanca dash velocidardesh*
	wire	fio	*feeoo*
	dynamo	dínamo	*deenamoo*
	bicycle trailer	atrelado para bicicleta	*atrellardoo parra beeceeclayta*
	frame	quadro	*cuardroo*
8	dress guard	protector (de vestuário)	*prootetor (duh veshtooaryoo)*
9	chain	corrente	*coorent*
	chain guard	caixa de corrente	*caisha duh coorent*
	chain lock	cadeado de corrente	*caddayardoo duh coorent*
	milometer	conta quilometros	*conta keelometroosh*
	child's seat	cadeira para criança	*caddayra parra criansa*
10	headlamp	farol	*faroll*
	bulb	lâmpada	*lamperdah*
11	pedal	pedal	*pedarl*
12	pump	bomba	*bomba*
13	reflector	reflector	*reflettor*
14	break pad	bloco de travão	*blocoo duh travow*
15	brake cable	cabo de travão	*carboo duh travow*
16	ring lock	cadeado de algema	*cadeeardoo duh aljayma*
17	carrier straps	elásticos de porta bagagem	*lashteecoosh duh porta bagarjaim*
	tachometer	velocimetro	*velossimetroo*
18	spoke	raio	*rayoo*
19	mudguard	guarda-lamas	*gwarda lamash*
20	handlebar	guiador	*guiadoor*
21	chain wheel	roda de lentes	*rodda duh lentesh*
	toe clip	gancho	*ganshoo*
22	crank axle	eixo de pedal	*aischoo duh pedarl*
	drum brake	jante	*jant*
23	valve	pipo de válvula	*peepoo duh valvoola*
24	valve tube	pipo de borracha	*peepoo duh borrasha*
25	gear cable	cabo de velocidades/ de engrenagem	*carboo duh velossidardesh/duh engrenarjaim*
26	fork	forqueta	*forketta*
27	front wheel	roda de frente	*rodda duh frent*
28	seat	selim	*selleem*

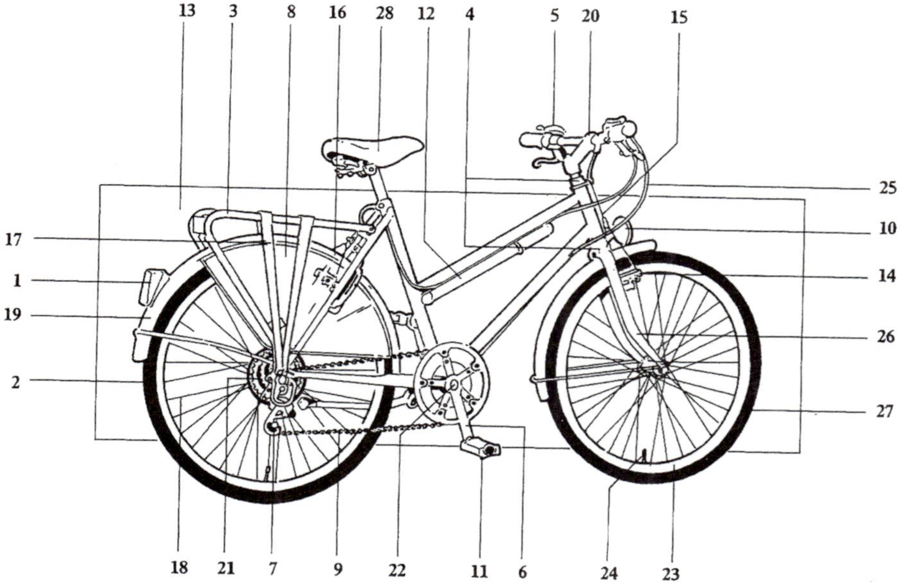
13
3
8
16
28
12
4
5
20
15
17
1
19
2
25
10
14
26
27
18
21
7
9
22
11
6
24
23

What time can I pick the...up tomorrow?	A que horas posso passar amanhã para vir buscar o/a ...? *ah kay orash possoo passar ahmarnyar parra veer booshcar oo/a ...?*
When does the...have to be back?	Quando tenho de vir entregar o/a ...? *cuarndoo tenyoo duh veer entreggar oo/a ...?*
Where's the petrol tank?	Onde está o depósito? *ond eshtah oo depozeetoo?*
What sort of fuel does it take?	Que tipo de combustível consome? *kuh teepoo duh combushteevel consom?*

5.10 Hitchhiking

Where are you heading?	Para onde vai? *parra ond vy?*
Can I come along?	Posso ir consigo? *possoo eer conseegoo?*
Can my boyfriend/ girlfriend come too?	O meu amigo/a minha amiga também pode ir? *oo mayoo ameegoo/ah meenya ameega tambaim pod eer?*
I'm trying to get to...	Vou para... *voe parra...*
Is that on the way to...?	Fica em caminho à...? *feeca aim cameenyoo ah...?*
Could you drop me off...?	Poderia deixar-me em...? *pooderia dayshar muh aim...?*
– here?	Poderia deixar-me aqui? *pooderia dayshar muh akee?*
– at the...exit?	Poderia deixar-me quando se corta para... *pooderia dayshar muh cuarndoo se corta parra...*
– in the centre?	Poderia deixar-me no centro? *pooderia dayshar muh noo centroo?*
– at the next roundabout?	Poderia deixar-me na próxima rotunda? *pooderia dayshar muh na prosseema rotoonda?*
Could you stop here, please?	Importa-se de parar aqui, se faz favor? *importas duh parar akee suh faj favvor?*
I'd like to get out here	Gostaria de descer aqui *gostaria duh deshsair akee*
Thanks for the lift	Muito obrigado pela boleia *mueentoo obrigahdoo pella boolay*

6

Public transport

6 Public transport

6.1 In general

● In addition to the rather sparse Portuguese rail network, there is a comprehensive long distance coach service with good connections between north Portugal and the Algarve and between most towns and cities. The Portuguese capital, Lisbon, is well-served by its bus network, taxis, river ferries, a small underground railway (undergoing expansion) and special lifts/funiculars for getting up and down the city's seven hills.

Announcements

O comboio para..., das 10:40 horas tem um atraso de 15 minutos	The 10:40 train to...has been delayed by 15 minutes
Na linha 5 vai chegar o comboio das 10:40 para.../de...	The train now arriving at platform 5 is the 10:40 train to.../from...
Da linha 5 vai sair o comboio das 10:40 para...	The 10:40 train to...is about to leave from platform 5
Estamos à chegar à estação...	We're now approaching... station

Where does this train go to?	Para onde vai este comboio? *parra ond vy esht comboyoo?*
Does this boat go to...?	Este barco vai para...? *esht barcoo vy parra...?*
Can I take this bus to...?	Posso tomar este autocarro para ir para...? *possoo toomar esht owtoocahroo parra eer parra...?*
Does this train stop at...?	Este comboio pára em...? *esht comboyoo para aim...?*
Is this seat taken/free/ reserved?	Este lugar está ocupado/livre/ reservado? *esht loogar eshtar ocoopardoo/ leevre/rezairvardoo?*
I've booked...	Reservei... *reservay...*
Could you tell me where I have to get off for... ?	Pode dizer-me onde devo sair para...? *pod deezair muh ond dayvoo sayeer parra...?*
Could you let me know when we get to...?	Podia avisar-me quando chegarmos a...? *poodia aveezar-muh cuarndoo shegarmoosh ah...?*
Could you stop at the next stop, please?	Podia parar na próxima paragem, se faz favor? *poodia parrar nah prosseema pararjaim, suh faj favvor?*

Where are we now?	Onde estamos? *ond eshtarmoosh?*
Do I have to get off here?	Tenho de sair aqui? *tenyoo duh sayeer akee*
Have we already passed...?	Já passámos por...? *jah passarmoosh por...*
How long have I been asleep?	Quanto tempo é que dormi? *cuarntoo tempoo eh kuh dormee?*
How long does... stop here?	Quanto tempo fica...aqui parado? *cuarntoo tempoo feeca...akee parardoo?*
Can I come back on the same ticket?	Também posso voltar com este bilhete? *tambaim possoo voltar com esht beelyet?*
Can I change on this ticket?	Posso mudar com este bilhete? *possoo moodar com est beelyet?*
How long is this ticket valid for?	Quanto tempo é que este bilhete é válido? *cuarntoo tempoo eh kuh esht beelyet eh vallydoo?*

6.2 Questions to passengers

Ticket types

Primeira ou segunda classe?	First or second class?
Só ida ou ida e volta?	Single or return?
Fumadores ou não?	Smoking or non-smoking?
Janela ou coxia?	Window or aisle?
A frente ou atrás?	Front or back?
Lugar sentado ou cama?	Seat or couchette?
Em cima, no meio ou em baixo?	Top, middle or bottom?
Turística ou primeira classe?	Tourist class or business class?
Camarote ou cadeira?	Cabin or seat?
Para pessoa só ou casal?	Single or double?
Quantas pessoas viajam?	How many are travelling?

Destination

Para onde deseja ir?	Where do you wish to go?
Quando deseja partir?	When do you wish to leave?
O seu...parte às...	Your...leaves at...
Tem de fazer transbordo	You have to change trains/ coaches
Tem de sair em...	You have to get off at...
Tem de fazer escala por...	You have to travel via...
A partida é no dia...	The outward journey is on...
O regresso é no dia...	The return journey is on...
Tem de estar a bordo das...no máximo	You have to be on board by...

O seu bilhete, se faz favor	Your ticket, please
A sua marcação, se faz favor	Your reservation, please
O seu passaporte, se faz favor	Your passport, please
Não está sentado no seu lugar	You're in the wrong seat
Está sentado no...errado	You're on/in the wrong...
Este lugar está reservado	This seat is reserved
Tem de pagar uma taxa	You'll have to pay a supplement
Tem um atraso de...minutos	There is a delay of... minutes

6.3 Tickets

Where can I...?	Onde é que posso...? *onde eh kuh possoo...?*
– buy a ticket?	Onde é que posso comprar um bilhete? *onde eh kuh possoo comprar oom beelyet?*
– make a reservation?	Onde é que posso reservar um lugar? *onde eh kuh possoo rezairvar oom loogar?*
– book a flight?	Onde é que posso marcar um vôo? *onde eh kuh possoo marcar oom voe?*
Could I have a...to..., please?	Queria um...para...? *kerria oom...para...?*
– a single	Queria um bilhete só de ida para...? *kerria oom beelyet soh duh eeda parra...?*
– a return	Queria um bilhete de ida e volta para...? *kerria oom beelyet duh eeda e volta parra...?*
first class	primeira classe *preemayra clahs*
second class	segunda classe *segoonda clahs*
tourist class	classe turística *clahs tooreeshteeca*
business class	classe de negócios *clahs duh negossyoosh*
I'd like to book a seat/couchette/cabin	Queria reservar um lugar/uma cama/um camarote *kerria rezairvar oom loogar/ooma camma/ oom cammarot*
I'd like to book a berth in the sleeping car	Queria reservar um lugar na carruagem-cama *kerria rezairvar oom loogar na carrooarjaim camma*
top/middle/bottom	em cima/no meio/em baixo *aim seema/noo mayoo/aim byshoo*
smoking/no smoking	fumadores/não fumadores *foomadoresh/now foomadoresh*
by the window	à janela *ah janella*

single/double — **individual/duplo** *indeeveedual/dooploo*

at the front/back — **à frente/atrás** *ah frent/ah traj*

There are...of us — **Somos...pessoas** *somush...pessoash*

a car — **um carro** *oom cahroo*

a caravan — **uma roulotte** *ooma roolot*

...bicycles — **...bicicletas** *...beeseeclaytash*

Do you also have...? — **Também tem...?** *tambaim taim...?*

– season tickets? — **Também tem um bilhete para várias viagens?** *tambaim taim oom beelyet parra varriash veearjainsh?*

– weekly tickets? — **Também tem passe semanal?** *tambaim taim pass semanal?*

– monthly tickets? — **Também tem um passe mensal?** *tambaim taim oom pass mensal?*

6.4 Information

Where...? — **Onde...?** *ond...?*

Where's the information desk? — **Onde são as informações?** *ond sow ash eenformasoynsh?*

Where can I find a timetable? — **Onde está o horário das partidas/chegadas?** *ond eshtah oo orareeoo dash parteedash/sheggardash?*

Where's the...desk? — **Onde é o guiché de...?** *ond eh oo geeshay duh...?*

Do you have a city map with the bus/the underground routes on it? — **Tem uma planta da cidade com a rede dos autocarros/do metropolitano?** *taim ooma planta dah sidarde com ah reyd dooz outoocahroosh/doo metropooleetarnoo?*

Do you have a timetable? — **Tem um horário?** *taim oom oraryoo?*

I'd like to confirm/cancel/change my booking for/trip to... — **Queria confirmar/anular/alterar a marcação/viagem para...** *kerria confeermar/anoolar/alterar ah marcasow/veearjaim parra...*

Will I get my money back? — **O dinheiro é devolvido?** *oo deenyayroo eh devolveedoo?*

I want to go to... How do I get there? (What's the quickest way there?) — **Tenho de ir para...Qual é a viagem (mais rápida) para lá?** *tenyoo duh eer parra...cuarl eh ah veearjaim (mysh rappida) parra la?*

How much is a single/return ticket to...? — **Quanto custa um bilhete de ida/ida e volta para...?** *cuarntoo cooshta oom beelyet duh eeda e volta parra...?*

Do I have to pay a supplement?	Tenho de pagar suplemento? *tenyoo duh paggar sooplementoo?*
Can I interrupt my journey with this ticket?	Com este bilhete, posso interromper a viagem? *com esht beelyet possoo eenterompair ah veearjaim?*
How much luggage am I allowed?	Quantos quilos de bagagem posso levar? *cuarntoosh keeloosh duh bagarjaim possoo levar?*
Can I send my luggage in advance?	Posso enviar a minha bagagem com antecedência? *possoo enviar a meenya bagarjaim com antessidencia?*
Does this...travel direct?	Este...é directo? *esht...eh deeretoo?*
Do I have to change? Where?	Tenho de fazer transbordo? Onde? *tenyoo duh fazair transhboordoo? ond?*
Will there be any stopovers?	O avião faz escalas? *oo avvyiow faj eshcarlash?*
Does the boat call in at any ports on the way?	O navio pára em alguns portos? *oo naveeoo para aim algoonsh portoosh?*
Does the train/ bus stop at...?	O comboio/camioneta pára em...? *oo comboyoo/camioonayta para aim...?*
Where should I get off?	Onde é que devo sair? *ond eh kuh dayvoo syeer?*
Is there a connection to...?	Há ligação para...? *ah leegasow parra...?*
How long do I have to wait?	Quanto tempo tenho de esperar? *cuarntoo tempoo tenyoo duh eshperrar?*
When does...leave?	Quando é que parte...? *cuarndoo eh kuh part...?*
What time does the first/next/last...leave?	A que horas é o primeiro/próximo/último...? *ah kay orash eh oo preemayroo/prosseemoo/oolteemoo...?*
How long does...take?	Quanto tempo leva...? *cuarntoo tempoo levva?*
What time does...arrive in...?	A que horas chega...a...? *ah kay orash shayga...ah...?*
Where does the...to... leave from?	Donde parte o...para...? *dond part oo...parra...?*
Is this...to...?	É este...para...? *eh esht...parra...?*

6.5 Aeroplanes

● **At a Portuguese airport** (*aeroporto*), you will find the following signs:

chegadas arrivals	voos domésticos domestic flights	alfândega customs
partidas departures	internacional international	

6.6 Trains

- **The Portuguese rail network** is still being developed and upgraded, but there are fast services between the main cities of Lisbon and Oporto

6.7 Taxis

- **Metered taxis** are available in all cities and large towns and are usually black and green. In the smaller towns, it is usual to agree a fixed price in advance as well as to check that the meter starts the journey at zero. A supplement is normally payable for luggage, a journey at night and on sundays or public holidays, but Portuguese taxis are generally cheaper than taxis in the rest of Europe.

livre for hire	ocupado booked	praça de táxis taxi rank

Taxi! ______ Táxi!
tarksy!

Could you get me a taxi, please? ______ Podia chamar um táxi?
poodia shammar oom tarksy?

Where can I find a taxi around here? ______ Onde é que posso apanhar um táxi, aqui perto?
ond eh kuh possoo apanyar oom tarksy akee pairtoo?

Could you take me to..., please? ______ Podia levar-me para..., se faz favor?
poodia levah muh parra..., suh faj favvor?

– this address ______ Podia levar-me para esta morada, se faz favor?
poodia levah muh parra eshta morrarda, suh faj favvor?

– the...hotel ______ Podia levar-me para o hotel..., se faz favor?
poodia levah muh parra oo ohtel..., suh faj favvor?

– the town/city centre ______ Podia levar-me para o centro, se faz favor?
poodia levah muh parra oo sentroo, suh faj favvor?

– the station ______ Podia levar-me para a estação, se faz favor?
poodia levah muh parra ah eshtasow, suh faj favvor?

– the airport ______ Podia levar-me ao aeroporto se faz favor?
poodia levah muh ow ayroopoortoo, suh faj favvor?

How much is the trip to...? ______ Qual é o preço da viagem para...?
cuarl eh oo praysoo dah veearjaim parra...?

How far is it to...? ______ Qual é a distância até...?
cuarl eh ah deeshtarnsia atay...?

Could you turn on the meter, please? ______ Pode ligar o taxímetro, se faz favor?
pod leegar oo tazkseemetroo, suh faj favvor?

I'm in a hurry	Estou com pressa *eshtoe com pressa*
Could you speed up/ slow down a little?	Podia guiar mais depressa/mais devagar? *poodia guiar mysh depressa/mysh deevagar?*
Could you take a different route?	Podia ir por outro caminho? *poodia eer por ohtroo cameenyoo?*
I'd like to get out here, please	Deixe-me ficar aqui, se faz favor *daysh muh feecar akee, suh faj favvor*
You have to go...here	Tem de ir aqui... *taim duh eer akee...*
You have to go straight on here	Tem de ir aqui em frente *taim duh eer akee aim frent*
You have to turn left here	Tem de ir aqui à esquerda *taim duh eer akee ah eshkairda*
You have to turn right here	Tem de ir aqui à direita *taim duh eer akee ah dirayta*
This is it	É aqui *eh akee*
Could you wait a minute for me, please?	Podia esperar um momento? *poodia eshperar oom moomentoo?*

7

Overnight accommodation

7 Overnight accommodation

7.1 General

- ***Hoteis (hotels):*** these are classified according to the standard of comfort offered and range from five star de luxe to simple one star, priced accordingly. The same applies to aparthotels and motels.
Pousadas: these are extremely well-appointed state-owned hotels located either in historic buildings or areas of particular natural beauty.
Estalagens: these are usually restored buildings similar to *pousadas* but privately owned and offering a good level of accommodation.
Habitacões de Turismo: these offer short-stay accommodation in large and beautiful private residences similar to stately homes. The owners are often present and the level of comfort varies.
Pensões, residências, albergarias: these are usually less expensive and offer a lesser degree of comfort than the other forms of accommodation. They are also classified and sometimes visitors to Portugal may fare better in a highly classified *residência* or *albergaria* than in a low rated hotel.
Camping: camping away from the one hundred or so designated camp sites is not usually allowed.
Albergos da juventude: there are very few youth hostels in Portugal. There is no upper age limit. Advance booking at peak times is advisable.

Quanto tempo quer ficar?	How long do you want to stay?
Preencha esta ficha, se faz favor	Fill out this form, please
Posso ver o seu passaporte?	Could I see your passport?
Tem de pagar um depósito	I'll need a deposit
Tem de pagar adiantado	You'll have to pay in advance

My name is... I've made a reservation (over the phone/by mail/by fax) — Chamo-me... Reservei um lugar/um quarto (pelo telefone/por escrito/por fax)
shammoo muh...rezervay om loogar/oom cuartoo (pelloo telefon/poor eshcreetoo/poor fax)

How much is it per night/week/month? — Qual é o preço por noite/por semana/por mês?
cuarl eh oo praysoo por noyt/por semarna/por mayge?

We'll be staying at least...nights/weeks — Ficamos pelo menos...noites/semanas
feecarmoosh pello menoosh... noytsh/semarnash

We don't know yet — Ainda não sabemos precisamente
ayeenda now sabbaymoosh preseezament

Do you allow pets (cats/dogs)? — É permitido trazer animais domésticos (cães/gatos)?
eh pairmeeteedo trazair aneemysh doomeshteecoosh (caynsh/gartoosh)?

Overnight accommodation

What time does the gate/door open/close?	A que horas abrem/fecham a cancela/a porta? *ah kay orash abraim/feysham ah cancella/ah porta?*
Could you get me a taxi, please?	Poderia mandar vir um táxi? *pooderia mandar veer oom tacksy?*
Is there any mail for me?	Há correio para mim? *ah coorayoo parra meem?*

7.2 Camping

See the diagram on page 69.

Pode escolher o seu lugar	You can pick your own site
Nós lhe indicamos um lugar	You'll be allocated a site
Este é o número do seu lugar	This is your site number
Importa-se de colar isto no seu carro?	Stick this on your car, please
Não perca este cartão	Please don't lose this card

Where's the manager?	Onde está o responsável? *ond eshtah oo reshponsarvel?*
Are we allowed to camp here?	Podemos acampar aqui? *poodaymoosh acampar akee?*
There are...of us and we have...tents	Somos...pessoas e temos...tendas *somoosh...pessoash e taymoosh...tendash*
Can we pick our own site?	Nós próprios podemos escolher um lugar? *nosh propreeoosh poodaymoosh eshcoolyair oom loogar?*
Do you have a quiet spot for us?	Poderia dar-nos um lugar tranquilo? *pooderia dar noosh oom loogar trankeeloo?*
Do you have any other pitches available?	Não tem um outro lugar livre? *now taim oom ohtroo loogar leevre?*
It's too windy/sunny/ shady here.	Aqui há muito vento/sol/muita sombra *akee ah mweentoo ventoo/sol/mweenta sombra*
It's very crowded here	Há muita gente *ah mweenta jent*
The ground's too hard/uneven	O chão aqui é muito duro/desigual *oo shau akee eh mueentoo dooroo/deseeguarl*
Do you have a level spot for the camper/ caravan/folding caravan?	Poderia arranjar um lugar plano para o reboque/a rulote/o trailer? *pooderia arranjar oom loogar plarnoo parra oo rabok/a roolot/oo trailer?*
Could we have adjoining pitches?	Podemos ficar juntos? *poodaymoosh feecar joontoosh?*
Can we park the car next to the tent?	Pode-se estacionar o carro perto da tenda? *pod suh eshtasionar oo cahroo pairtoo da tenda?*

How much is it per person/tent/caravan/car? — **Quanto custa por pessoa/tenda/rulote/carro?**
cuarntoo cooshta por pessoah/tenda/roolot/cahroo?

Are there any...? — **Há...?**
ah...?

– hot showers? — **Há duches com água quente?**
ah dooshesh com agwa kent?

– washing machines? — **Há máquinas de lavar?**
ah markeenash duh lavar?

Is there a...on the site? — **Há neste parque um...?**
ah nesht park oom...?

Is there a children's play area on the site? — **Há neste parque um jardim infantil?**
ah nesht park oom jardeem eenfanteel?

Are there covered cooking facilities on the site? — **Há neste parque um lugar coberto para cozinhar?**
ah nesht park oom loogar coobairtoo parra coozeenyar?

Can I rent a safe here? — **Posso alugar um cofre?**
possoo alloogar oom cofre?

Are we allowed to barbecue here? — **Pode-se fazer churrasco aqui?**
pod suh fazair choorashcoo akee?

Are there any power points? — **Há tomadas de corrente eléctrica?**
ha toomardash duh corrent eeletreeca?

Is there drinking water? — **Há água potável?**
ah agwa pootarvel?

When's the rubbish collected? — **Quando recolhem o lixo?**
cuarndoo recolyaim oo leeshoo?

Do you sell gas bottles (butane gas/ propane gas)? — **Vende garrafas de gás (butagás/gás propano)?**
vende garrafash duh gaj (bootagaj/gaj prooparnoo)?

7.3 Hotel/B&B/apartment/holiday house

Do you have a single/double room available? — **Tem um quarto simples/de casal livre?**
taim oom cuartoo seemplesh/duh cazal leevre?

How much is it per person/per room? — **Qual é o preço por pessoa/por quarto?**
cuarl eh oo praysoo por pessoa/por cuartoo?

Does that include breakfast/lunch/dinner? — **Já está incluido pequeno almoço/almoço/jantar?**
jah eshtah eenclooeedoo peekaynoo almohsoo/almohsoo/jantar?

Could we have two adjoining rooms? — **Pode arranjar dois quartos juntos?**
pod arranjar doysh cuartoosh joontoosh?

I'd like a room with/ without toilet/bath/ shower — **Queria um cuarto com/sem casa de banho/banheira/duche individual**
kerria oom cuartoo com/saim carza duh barnyoo/banyayra/doosh eendeeveedual

I'd like a room (not) facing the street — **Queria um cuarto (não) para o lado da rua**
kerria oom cuartoo (now) parra oo lardoo da rooah

I'd like a room with/ without a view of the sea	Queria um cuarto com/sem vista para o mar *kerria oom cuartoo com/saim veeshta parra oo mar*
Is there...in the hotel?	O hotel tem... *o ohtel taim...*
Is there a lift in the hotel?	O hotel tem elevador? *oo ohtel taim eelevadoor?*
Do you have room service?	O hotel tem serviço de quarto? *oo ohtel taim serveesoo duh cuartoo?*
Could I see the room?	Posso ver o quarto? *possoo vair oo cuartoo?*
I'll take this room	Fico com este quarto *feecoo com esht cuartoo*
We don't like this one	Este não nos agrada *esht now noos agrarda*
Do you have a larger/ less expensive room?	Tem um quarto maior/mais barato? *taim oom cuartoo myor/mysh barartoo?*
Could you put in a cot?	Poderia pôr aqui uma cama de criança? *pooderia poor akee ooma carma duh creeansa?*
What time's breakfast?	A que horas servem o pequeno almoço? *ah kay orash servaim oo peekaynoo almohsoo?*
Where's the dining room?	Onde é a sala de jantar? *ond eh a sarla duh jantar?*
Can I have breakfast in my room?	Posso tomar o pequeno almoço no quarto? *possoo toomar oo peekaynoo almohsoo noo cuartoo?*
Where's the emergency exit/fire escape?	Onde fica a saída de emergência/escada de incêndio? *ond feeca ah sayeeda duh emergensia/eshcarda duh eensendeeoo?*
Where can I park my car (safely)?	Onde há um lugar (seguro) para estacionar o meu carro? *ond ah oom loogar (segooroo) parra eshtassionar oo mayoo karoo?*
The key to room..., please	A chave do quarto..., se faz favor *a sharv doo cuartoo..., suh faj favvor*
Could I put this in your safe, please?	Posso pôr isto no seu cofre? *possoo poor eeshtoo noo sayoo cofre?*

Os lavabos e o duche ficam no mesmo andar/no seu quarto	You can find the toilet and shower on the same floor/in your room
Por este lado	This way
O seu quarto é no...andar	Your room is on the...floor
O número é...	It's number is...

Camping equipment

(the diagram shows the numbered parts)

	luggage space	parte resguardo para	*part reshgwardoo parra*
		a bagagem	*ah bagarjaim*
	can opener	abre-latas	*abre lartash*
	butane gas	garrafa de gás	*garrafa duh gaj*
	bottle	saco para bicicleta	*sarcoo parra*
			beeceeclayta
1	pannier	fogão de campismo	*foogow duh campeejmoo*
2	primus stove	oleado	*olliardoo*
3	groundsheet	martelo	*martelloo*
	mallet	rede	*reyd*
	hammock	jerrican	*gerrican*
4	jerry can	fogueira	*foogayra*
	campfire	cadeira dobrável	*cadayra doobrarvel*
5	folding chair	geladeira	*geladayra*
6	insulated picnic	almofadas de	*almoofardash*
	box	geladeira	*duh geladayra*
	ice pack	bússola	*boosolla*
	compass	camisa	*cameeza*
	wick	saca-rolhas	*saca rolyash*
	corkscrew	cama inflável	*carma eenflarvel*
7	airbed	pipo	*peepoo*
8	airbed plug	bomba de ar	*bomba di ar*
	pump	toldo	*toldoo*
9	awning	tapete	*tappett*
10	karimat	panela	*panella*
11	pan	asa de panela	*arza duh panella*
12	pan handle	feixo	*fayshoo*
	zip	mochila	*mosheela*
13	backpack	espia	*eshpeea*
14	guy rope	saco de dormir	*sarcoo duh dormeer*
	sleeping bag	lanterna	*lantairna*
15	storm lantern	cama de campismo	*carma duh campeejmoo*
	camp bed	mesa	*mayza*
	table	tenda	*tenda*
16	tent	cavilha	*caveelya*
17	tent peg	estaca da tenda	*eshtarca da tenda*
18	tent pole	termos	*termoosh*
	vacuum flask	cantil	*canteel*
19	water bottle	mola da roupa	*molla da roepa*
	clothes peg	arame	*ararm*
	clothes line	pára-vento	*parra ventoo*
	windbreak	lanterna de bolso	*lantairna duh bolsoo*
20	torch	canivete	*cannivet*
	pocket knife		

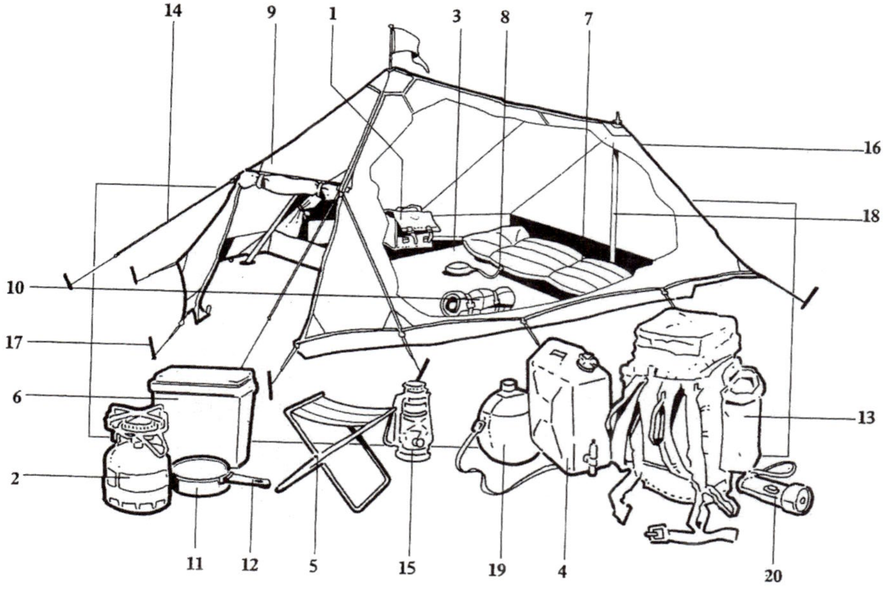
14
9
1
3
8
7
16
18
10
17
6
13
2
11
12
5
15
19
4
20

Could you wake me at...tomorrow?	Poderia acordar-me amanhã às ...? *pooderia acordar muh armanyar ash ...?*
Could you find a babysitter for me?	Poderia ajudar-me a arranjar uma pessoa para tomar conta do bébé? *pooderiah ajoodar muh ah arranjar ooma pessoa parra toomar conta do baybay?*
Can I have an extra blanket?	Arranja-me um outro cobertor, se faz favor? *arranj muh oom ohtroo coobertor, suh faj favvor?*
What days do the cleaners come in?	Em que dia fazem a limpeza? *aim kuh deeah farzaim uh leempayza?*
When are the sheets/ towels/tea towels changed?	Quando é que são mudados os lençóis/as toalhas/os panos de cozinha? *cuarndoo eh kuh sow moodardash oosh lensoysh/ash tooalyash/oosh parnoosh duh coozeenya?*

7.4 Complaints

We can't sleep because of the noise	Não conseguimos dormir devido ao barulho *now consegeemoosh doormeer deveedoo ow baroolyoo*
Could you turn the radio down, please?	Pode pôr o rádio um pouco mais baixo? *pod poor oo rardeeoo oom pohcoo maiz abyshoo?*
We're out of toilet paper	Acabou-se o papel higiénico *acarboe suh oo papell eegenneecoo*
There isn't any.../there's not enough...	Não há.../não há...suficiente *now ah.../now ah...soofeecient*
The bed linen's dirty	A roupa de cama está suja *a roepa duh carma eshtah sooja*
The room hasn't been cleaned	O quarto não foi limpo *oo cuartoo now foy leempoo*
The kitchen is not clean	A cozinha não foi limpa *a coozeenya now foy leempa*
The kitchen utensils are dirty	Os utensílios de cozinha estão sujos *ooz ootenseelyoosh duh cozeenya eshtow soojoosh*
The heater's not working	O aquecimento não funciona *oo akessimentoo now fooncyonna*
There's no (hot) water/electricity	Não há água (quente)/electricidade *now ah agwa (kent)/eeletreecidard*
...is broken	...está estragado *...eshtah eshtragardoo*
Could you have that seen to?	Poderia mandar arranjar? *pooderia mandar arranjar?*
Could I have another room/site?	Poderia arranjar um outro quarto/lugar para a tenda? *pooderia arranjar oom ohtroo cuartoo/loogar parra a tenda*
The bed creaks terribly	A cama faz muito barulho *a cahma faj mweentoo baroolyoo*
The bed sags	A cama baixa muito no meio *a cahma bysha mweentoo no mayoo*

There are bugs/insects	Há muitos bichos/insectos *ah mweentoosh beeshoosh/eensectoosh*
This place is full of mosquitos	Isto está cheio de mosquitos *eeshtoo eshtah shayoo duh moshkeetsch*
– cockroaches	Isto está cheio de baratas *eeshtoo eshtah shayoo duh barattash*

7.5 Departure

See also 8.2 Settling the bill

I'm leaving tomorrow. Could I settle my bill, please?	Saio amanhã. Posso pagar agora? *sayoo armanyar. possoo paggar agoara?*
What time should we vacate?	A que horas temos de deixar...? *a kay orash taymoosh duh dayshar...?*
Could I have my deposit/passport back?	Pode devolver-me o depósito/o meu passaporte? *pod devolvair muh oo deposeetoo/oo mayoo passaport?*
We're in a terrible hurry	Estamos com muita pressa *eshtarmoosh com mueenta pressa*
Could you forward my mail to this address?	Poderia enviar-me o correio para esta morada? *pooderia enviar muh oo corrayoo parra eshta morarda?*
Could we leave our luggage here until we leave?	Podemos deixar as malas aqui até irmos embora? *poodaymoosh dayshar ash malash akee atay eermoosh emboora?*
Thank you very much for your hospitality	Muito obrigado pela hospitalidade *mweentoo obrigahdoo pella oshpeetalidade*

Money matters

8

8 Money matters

● **In general,** banks in Portugal are open to the public between 8.30am and 3pm, Monday to Friday, but closing times may vary and smaller branches may close for lunch. The sign *câmbio* indicates that foreign currency may be exchanged and proof of identity, usually in the form of a passport, will be required by Portuguese banks. Hotels will usually change money but at less favourable rates. Portugal has a large network of cash machines outside the banks and by using a UK-issued PIN number, money changing is very quick and simple.

8.1 Banks

Where can I find a bank/an exchange office around here? — Onde é que há um banco/uma casa de câmbio por aqui?
ond eh kuh ah oom bancoo/ooma carza duh cambyoo poor akee?

Where can I cash this traveller's cheque/giro cheque? — Onde posso trocar este traveller cheque/cheque do correio?
ond possoo troocar esht traveller shek/shek doo coorayoo?

Can I cash this...here? — Posso trocar este...aqui?
possoo troocar esht...akee?

Can I withdraw money on my credit card here? — Posso levantar dinheiro aqui com um cartão de crédito?
possoo levantar deenyayroo akee com oom cartow duh credeetoo?

What's the minimum/maximum amount? — Qual é o mínimo/máximo?
cuarl eh oo meeneemoo/masseemoo?

Can I take out less than that? — Também posso levantar menos?
tambaim possoo levantar menoosh?

I've had some money transferred here. Has it arrived yet? — Pedi uma transferência telegráfica. Já chegou?
pedee ooma transhferensia telegraffeeca. Jah shegoe?

These are the details of my bank in the UK — Estes são os dados do meu banco na Grã Bretanha
eshtesh sow oosh dardoosh doo mayoo bancoo nah grar bretarnya

This is my bank/giro number — Este é o número da minha conta bancária/no correio
esht eh oo noomeroo da meenya conta bancaria/noo coorayoo

I'd like to change some money — Eu gostarià de trocar dinheiro
eyoo goshtaria duh troocar deenyayroo

– pounds into... — Eu gostarià de trocar libras esterlinas por...
eyoo goshtaria duh troocar leebrash eshterleenash por...

– dollars into... — Eu gostarià de trocar dólares americanos por...
eyoo goshtaria duh troocar dollaresh amereecarnoosh por...

What's the exchange rate? — Qual é o câmbio?
cuarl eh oo carmbio?

Could you give me some small change?	Podia dar-me também dinheiro trocado, por favor? *poodia dar muh tambaim deenyayroo troocardoo por favvor?*
This is not right	Isto está errado *eeshtoo eshtah eerardoo*

Tem de assinar aqui	You have to sign here
Tem de preencher isto	You have to fill this out
Mostra-me o seu passaporte?	Could I see your passport?
Mostra-me o seu bilhete de identidade?	Could I see some identification?
Mostra-me o seu cartão dos correios?	Could I see your girobank card?
Mostra-me o seu cartão do banco?	Could I see your bank card?

8.2 Settling the bill

Could you put it on my bill?	Pode enviar para a minha conta? *pod enviar parra ah meenya conta?*
Does this amount include service?	O serviço está incluído? *oo sairveesoo schtah eenclooeedoo?*
Can I pay by...?	Posso pagar com...? *possoo paggar com...?*
Can I pay by credit card?	Posso pagar com um cartão de crédito? *possoo paggar com oom cartow duh craydeetoo?*
Can I pay by traveller's cheque?	Posso pagar com um traveller cheque? *possoo pagar com oom traveller shek?*
Can I pay with foreign currency?	Posso pagar com moeda estrangeira? *possoo paggar com mooayda eshtranjayra?*
You've given me too much/you haven't given me enough change	Deu-me dinheiro a mais/menos *dayoo muh deenyayroo ah mysh/menoosh*
Would you like to check the bill again?	Quer verificar a conta novamente? *care vereefeecar ah conta novvamentjee?*
Could I have a receipt?	Pode dar-me um recibo/talão da caixa? *pod dar muh oom resseeboo/talow da caisha?*
I don't have enough money on me	Não tenho comigo dinheiro suficiente *now tenyoo comeegoo deenyayroo soofeecient*
This is for you	Faça favor, isto é para si *fassa favvor eeshtoo eh parra see*

Não se aceita cartões de crédito/traveller cheques/moeda estrangeira	Credit cards/traveller's cheques/foreign currency are not accepted

Post and telephone

9

9 Post and telephone

9.1 Post

● **Most post offices** *(correios)* are open from 9am to 5pm from Monday to Friday and until 1pm on Saturdays. Some smaller post offices close for lunch between 12.30pm and 2.30pm. Stamps *(selos)* are also sold in tobacconists' shops *(tabacarias)* displaying the sign *CTT selos.* Portuguese postboxes are red.

vales postais money orders	telegramas telegrams	selos stamps
encomendas parcels		

Where's...?	Onde é...? *ond eh...?*
Where's the post office?	Onde é o correio mais perto? *ond eh oo coorayoo mysh pairtoo?*
Where's the main post office?	Onde é a agência principal do correio? *ond eh a ajencia preenceepal doo coorayoo?*
Where is the postbox?	Há aqui perto uma caixa de correio? *ah akee pairtoo ooma caisha duh coorayoo?*
Which counter is for...?	Qual é o guiché para...? *cuarl eh oo geeshay para...?*
– sending a fax?	Qual é o guiché para enviar um fax? *cuarl eh oo geeshay parra enviar oom fax?*
– changing money?	Qual é o guiché para trocar dinheiro? *cuarl eh oo geeshay parra troocar deenyayroo?*
– giro cheques?	Qual é o guiché para os cheques `giro'? *cuarl eh oo geeshay parra oosh sheksh jeero?*
– money orders?	Qual é o guiché para vale telegráfico? *cuarl eh oo geeshay parra val telegrarfeecoo?*
Poste restante	Posta-restante *poshta reshtant*
Is there any mail for me?	Há correio para mim? *ah coorayoo parra meem.*
My name's...	O meu nome é... *Oo mayoo nom eh...*

Stamps

What's the postage for a...to...?	Quanto custa um/uma...para...? *cuarntoo cooshta oom/ooma...parra...?*
Are there enough stamps on it?	Este valor de selos chega? *esht valor duh seloosh shayga?*
I'd like...stamps of...escudos	Queria...selos de...escudos *kerria...seloosh duh...eshcoodoosh*
I'd like to send this...	Queria enviar isto... *kerria enviar eeshtoo...*

– by express ___________ **Queria enviar isto por expresso**
kerria enviar eeshtoo poor eshpraysoo

– by air mail ___________ **Queria enviar isto por correio aéreo**
kerria enviar eeshtoo por coorayoo airayoo

– by registered mail ______ **Queria enviar isto registado**
kerria enviar eeshtoo regeeshtardoo

Telegram/fax

I'd like to send a telegram to... ________ **Queria enviar um telegrama para...**
kerria enviar oom telegrarma parra...

How much is it per word? _______ **Quanto custa cada palavra?**
cuarntoo cooshta cadda palarvra?

This is the text I want to send ______ **Este é o texto que quero enviar**
esht eh oo teshtoo kuh kerria enviar

Shall I fill out the form myself? _____ **Posso preencher eu próprio o impresso?**
possoo pre-enshair eyoo propreeoo oo eempraysoo?

Can I make photocopies/send a fax here? ___ **Posso fazer fotocópias/enviar um fax aqui?**
possoo fazair fotoocopiash/enviar oom fax akee?

How much is it per page? ___________ **Quanto custa por página?**
cuarntoo cooshta por parjeena?

9.2 Telephone

See also 1.8 Telephone alphabet

● **As in most** countries, telephone calls made from hotels are expensive. Most public telephones offer a direct international service, but as only low value coins can be used, a considerable quantity must be on hand. Cardphones are available and phone cards *(cartão credifone)* can be purchased from post offices. Portugal is well-served by the global mobile telephone network (GSM) and so it is well worth taking one along. Unlike in the UK, it is perfectly in order to ring someone after 9.30pm.

Is there a phone box around here? ______ **Há aqui perto uma cabine telefónica?**
ah akee pairtoo ooma cabeen telefoneeca?

Could I use your phone, please? _________ **Posso utilizar o seu telefone, se faz favor?**
possoo ooteeleezar oo sayoo telefon, suh faj favvor?

Do you have a (city/region)...phone directory? ___________ **Tem uma lista telefónica de.../da zona de...?**
taim ooma leeshta telefoneeca duh.../duh zona duh...?

Where can I get a phone card? ________ **Onde é que posso comprar um cartão credifone?**
ond eh kuh possoo comprar oom cartow credifon?

Could you tell me...?______ **Podia dizer-me...?**
poodia deezair muh...?

– the number for international directory enquiries?	Podia dizer-me o número das informações internacionais? *poodia deezair muh oo noomeroo daz eenformasoynsh eenternacionysh?*
– the number of room...?	Podia dizer-me o número do quarto...? *poodia deezair muh oo noomeroo doo cuartoo...?*
– the international access code?	Podia dizer-me o indicativo de acesso? *poodia deezair muh oo eendeecateevoo duh assesoo?*
– the country code for...?	Podia dizer-me o indicativo de...? *poodia deezair muh oo eendeecateevoo duh...?*
– the trunk code for...?	Podia dizer-me o indicativo da zona de...? *poodia deezair muh oo eendeecateevoo da zona duh...?*
– the number of...?	Podia dizer-me o número do assinante...? *poodia deezair muh oo noomeroo doo asseenant...?*
Could you check if this number's correct?	Podia verificar se este número está correcto? *poodia vereefeecar see esht noomeroo eshtah cooretoo?*
Can I dial international direct?	Posso telefonar directamente para o estrangeiro? *possoo telefonar deeretament parra oo eshtranjayroo?*
Do I have to go through the switchboard?	Tenho de pedir a chamada à telefonista? *tenyoo de pedeer a shamarda ah telefoneeshta?*
Do I have to dial '0' first?	Tenho de ligar primeiro o zero? *tenyoo de leegar preemayroo oo zayroo?*
Do I have to book my call?	Tenho de pedir a chamada? *tenyoo de pedeer ah shamarda?*
Could you dial this number for me?	Podia ligar para este número? *poodia leegar parra esht noomeroo?*
Could you put me through to.../extension...?	Podia ligar-me com.../a extensão...? *poodia leegar muh com.../ah eshtensow...?*
I'd like to place a reverse-charge call to...	Queria fazer uma chamada paga para... *kerria fazair ooma shamarda parga parra...?*
What's the charge per minute?	Quanto custa por minuto? *cuarntoo cooshta poor meenootoo?*
Have there been any calls for me?	Alguém telefonou para mim? *algaim telefonoe parra meem?*

The conversation

Hello, this is...	Está? Daqui fala... *eshtah? Dakee fala...*
Who is this, please?	Quem fala, se faz favor? *caim fala, suh faj favvor?*
Is this...?	Estou a falar com...? *eshtoe a falar com...?*

I'm sorry, I've dialled the wrong number	Desculpe, enganei-me no número *deshcoolp, enganay muh noo noomeroo*
I didn't understand what you said	Não compreendi o que disse *now compreyendee oo kuh deece*
I'd like to speak to...	Gostava de falar com... *goshtarva duh falar com...*
Is there anybody who speaks English?	Há alguém que fale inglês? *ah algaim kuh fala inglaij?*
Extension..., please	Extensão..., se faz favor *eshtensow..., seh faj favvor*
Could you ask him/her to call me back?	Podia pedir-lhe para me telefonar? *poodia peddeer lya parra muh telefonar?*
My name's... My number's...	O meu nome é... O meu número é... *oo mayoo nom eh... oo meu noomeroo eh...*
Could you tell him/her I called?	Podia dizer-lhe que eu telefonei? *poodia deezair lya kuh eyoo telefonay*
I'll call back tomorrow	Volto a telefonar-lhe amanhã *voltoo ah telefonar lya armanyar*

Telefone para o senhor/a senhora	There's a phone call for you
Ligue primeiro o zero	You have to dial '0' first
Aguarde um momento	One moment, please
Ninguém atende	There's no answer
O número está impedido	The line's engaged
Podia esperar?	Could you hold?
Vou ligar	Putting you through
O número não está correcto	You've got the wrong number
Ele/ela não está neste momento	He's/she's not here right now
Ele/ela volta...	He'll/she'll be back...
Está ligado ao receptor automático	This is the answering machine of...

Shopping

10

10 Shopping

● **Opening times:** Monday to Friday from 9am to 1pm and 3 to 7pm. On Saturdays shops close at 1pm, but there is a growing trend towards staying open in the afternoons. Shopping centres *(centro comercial)* are also open on Sundays and public holidays from 9am to 1pm, with longer opening hours towards Christmas. Some small shops stay open all day on Sundays. Supermarkets *(supermercado)* stay open until at least 10pm. Chemists' *(farmácia)* opening hours are the same as those of shops and the names of late-night duty chemists are displayed in the shop window and in the newspapers.

loja de antiguidades	antique shop
armazém	department store
artigos de desporto	sports shop
artigos dietéticos	health-food
artigos de segunda mão	second-hand goods
artigos fotográficos	camera shop
auto-serviço	self-service
cabeleireiro	hairdresser
casa de bicicletas	bicycle shop
casa de brinquedos	toy shop
casa de móveis	furniture shop
casa de vinhos	off-licence
centro comercial	shopping centre
decoração de interiores	interior design
delicatessen	delicatessen
discoteca/artigos musicais	record shop
drogaria	hardware shop
electrodomésticos	electrical appliances
farmácia	pharmacy/ dispensing chemist
feira	fleamarket
florista	florist's
frutaria	greengrocer's
geladaria	ice-cream parlour
joalharia	jewellery shop
lavandaria	launderette/ laundry
leitaria	dairy products shop
limpeza a seco	dry-cleaner's
livraria	bookshop
loja	shop
loja de modas	dress shop
loja de recordações	souvenir shop
mercado	market
mercearia	grocery store
óptica	optician's
padaria	bakery
pastelaria	cake shop
peixaria	fishmonger
perfumaria	perfumery
quiosque	kiosk
reparação de bicicletas	bicycle repairs
retrosaria	drapers
salão de beleza	beauty parlour
sapataria	shoe shop
sapateiro	cobbler
supermercado	supermarket
tabacaria	tobacconist's
talho	butcher's

10.1 Shopping conversations

Where can I get...?	Em que loja posso arranjar...? *aim kay lohja possoo arranjar...?*
When does this shop open?	Quando é que esta loja está aberta? *cuarndoo eh kuh eshta lohja eshtah aberta?*
Could you tell me where the...department is?	Poderia dizer-me onde fica a secção de...? *pooderia deezer muh ond feeca ah secksow duh...?*
Could you help me? I'm looking for...	Pode atender-me? Procuro...? *pod atendair muh? Procooroo...?*
Do you sell English/ American newspapers?	Tem jornais ingleses? *taim jornysh inglayzesh?*

Já está a ser atendido?	Are you being served?

No. I'd like...	Não. Queria... *now. Kerria...*
I'm just looking, if that's all right	Só estou a ver, obrigado *soh eshtoe a vair, obrigahdoo*

Mais alguma coisa?	Anything else?

Yes, I'd also like...	Sim, dê-me também... *seem, day muh tambaim...*
No, thank you. That's all	Não, muito obrigado. É tudo *now mueento obrigahdoo. Eh toodoo*
Could you show me..., please?	Pode deixar-me ver..., se faz favor? *pod dayshar muh vair..., suh faj favvor?*
I'd prefer...	Eu preferia... *eyoo prefferia...*
This is not what I'm looking for	Isto não é o que eu procuro *eeshtoo now eh oo kuh eyoo procooroo*
Thank you. I'll keep looking	Muito obrigado. Vou dar mais uma volta *mweentoo obrigahdoo. voe dar maiz ooma volta*
Do you have something...?	Não tem nada mais...? *now taim narda mysh...?*
– cheaper?	Não tem nada mais barato? *now taim narda mysh barartoo?*
– smaller?	Não tem nada mais pequeno? *now taim narda mysh peekaynoo?*
– larger?	Não tem nada maior? *now taim narda myor?*
I'll take this one/these	Levo este(s)/esta(s) *levoo esht (esh)/eshta (sh)*

Does it come with instructions?	O modo de emprego está lá dentro? *oo modoo di empraygoo eshtah la dentroo?*
It's too expensive	Acho demasiado caro *achoo demaziardoo caroo*
I'll give you...	Ofereço-lhe... *oferessoo lya...*
Could you keep this for me? I'll come back for it later	Importa-se de me guardar isto? Volto já a buscar *eemporta suh duh muh gwardar eeshtoo? Voltoo jah booshcar*
Have you got a bag?	Tem um saco? *taim oom sarcoo?*
Could you giftwrap it, please?	Pode embrulhar como prenda, se faz favor? *pod embrulyar comoo prenda, suh faj favvor?*

Lamento, mas não temos	I'm sorry, we don't have that
Lamento, já não temos mais	I'm sorry, we're sold out
Lamento, só vamos receber isso dentro de...	I'm sorry, that won't be in until...
Pode pagar na caixa	You can pay at the cash desk
Não aceitamos cartões de crédito	We don't accept credit cards
Não aceitamos traveller cheques	We don't accept traveller's cheques
Não aceitamos moedas estrangeiras	We don't accept foreign currency

10.2 Food

I'd like a hundred grams of...	Eu queria cem gramas de... *eyoo kerria saim grarmash duh ...*
– five hundred grams/ half a kilo of...	Eu queria meio quilo de... *eyoo kerria mayoo keeloo duh...*
– a kilo of...	Eu queria um quilo de... *eyoo kerria oom keeloo duh...*
Could you...?	Importa-se de...? *eemporta suh duh...?*
Could you slice it/ dice it, please?	Importa-se de cortar em fatias/bocados, se faz favor? *eemporta suh duh cortar aim fateeash/boocardoosh, suh faj favvor?*
Could you grate it, please?	Importa-se de o ralar, se faz favor? *eemporta suh duh oo rallar, suh faj favvor?*
Can I order it?	Posso encomendar? *possoo aincoomendar?*
I'll pick it up tomorrow/ at...	Venho buscar amanhã/às...horas *venyoo booshcar armanyar/ush...orash*

Can you eat/drink this?	Pode-se comer/beber? *pod se coomair/bebbair*
What's in it?	De que é feito? *duh kee eh faytoo?*

10 .3 Clothing and shoes

I saw something in the window. Shall I point it out?	Vi uma coisa na montra. Posso lhe mostrar? *vee ooma coyza na montra. possoo lya mooshtrar?*
I'd like something to go with this	Queria uma coisa para condizer com isto *kerria ooma coyza parra condeezair com eeshtoo*
Do you have shoes in this same colour?	Tem sapatos nesta mesma cor? *taim sapartoosh neshta mejma cor?*
I'm a size...in the UK	Na Grã Bretanha o meu número é... *na grar bretarnya oo mayoo noomeroo eh...*
Can I try this on?	Posso experimentar? *possoo eshprimentar?*
Where's the fitting room?	Onde fica o gabinete de prova? *ond feeca oo gabeenet duh provva?*
It doesn't fit	Não me serve *now muh sairve*
This is the right size	Esta medida é boa *eshta medeeda eh boa*
It doesn't suit me	Não me fica bem *now muh feeca baim*
Do you have this/these in...?	Tem também isto em... *taim tambaim eeshtoo aim...*
I find the heel too high/low	Acho o salto demasiado alto/baixo *ashoo oo saltoo demaziardoo altoo/byshoo*
Is this genuine leather?	Isto é couro verdadeiro? *eeshtoo eh cooroo verdadayroo?*
I'm looking for a... for a...-year-old baby/child	Procuro um...para um bébé/uma criança de...anos *procooroo oom...parra oom baybay/ooma criansa duh...arnoosh*
I'd prefer a...of...	Eu preferia um...de... *eyoo prefferia oom...duh...*
– silk	Eu preferia um...de seda *eyoo prefferia oom...duh sayda*
– cotton	Eu preferia um...de algodão *eyoo prefferia oom...duh algoodow*
– wool	Eu preferia um...de lã *eyoo prefferia oom... duh lang*
– linen	Eu preferia um...de linho *eyoo prefferia oom...duh leenyoo*
What temperature can I wash it at?	A que temperatura é que posso lavar? *a kay temperatoora eh kuh possoo lavar?*
Will it shrink in the wash?	Encolhe ao lavar? *aincollye ow lavar?*

Não passar a ferro	Pendurar molhado	Lavar à mão
Do not iron	Drip dry	Hand wash
Não centrifugar	Limpar a seco	Lavar à máquina
Do not spin dry	Dry clean	Machine wash

At the cobbler's

Could you mend these shoes?	Pode arranjar-me estes sapatos? *pod arranjar muh eshtash sapartoosh?*
Could you put new soles/heels on these?	Poderia pôr aqui solas novas/saltos novos? *pooderia poor akee solash novash/saltoosh novoosh?*
When will they be ready?	Quando estão prontos? *cuarndoo eshtow prontoosh?*
I'd like...	Eu queria... *eyoo kerria...*
– a tin of shoe polish	Eu queria uma caixa de pomada *eyoo kerria ooma caisha duh poomarda*
– a pair of shoelaces	Eu queria um par de atacadores *eyoo kerria oom par duh attackadooresh*

10.4 Photographs and video

I'd like a film for this camera, please	Eu queria um rolo para esta máquina, se faz favor *eyoo kerria oom rolloo parra eshta markina, suh faj favvor*
– a cartridge	Eu queria uma cassette *eyoo kerria ooma cassett*
– a slide film	Eu queria um rolo de diapositivos *eyoo kerria oom rolloo duh diaposeeteevoosh*
– a film cartridge	Eu queria um cassette para filmar *eyoo kerria oom cassett parra feelmar*
– a videotape	Eu queria um cassette de vídeo *eyoo kerria oom cassett duh veedyoo*
– a colour/black and white film	Eu queria um rolo a cores/a preto e branco *eyoo kerria oom rolloo ah cooresh/ah praytoo e brancoo*
– a super eight film	Eu queria um filme super de 8mm *eyoo kerria oom feelm soopair duh 8mm*
– a 12/24/36 exposures film	Eu queria um rolo de 12/24/36 fotografias *eyoo kerria oom rolloo duh 12/24/36 fotografeeash*
– a film of...ASA	Eu queria um rolo de ISO... *eyoo kerria oom rolloo duh ee ess oo...*
– a daylight film	Eu queria um rolo para luz natural *eyoo kerria oom rollo parra looj naturarl*
– a film for artificial light	Eu queria um rolo para luz artificial *eyoo kerria oom rolloo parra looj artifeeciarl*

Problems

Could you load the film for me?	Importa-se de colocar o rolo na máquina? *eemporta suh duh coloocar oo rolloo na markina?*
Could you take the film out for me?	Importa-se de tirar o rolo da máquina? *eemporta suh duh teerar oo rolloo da markina?*
Should I replace the batteries?	Tenho de substituir as pilhas? *tenyoo duh soobshteetweer ash peelyash?*
Could you have a look at my camera? It's not working	Importa-se de ver a minha máquina/câmara? Não trabalha *eemporta suh duh vair a meenya markina/camera? Now trabalya*
The...is broken	O...está estragado *oo...eshtah eshtragardoo*
The film's jammed	O rolo está preso *oo rolloo eshtah prayzoo*
The film's broken	O rolo está partido *oo rolloo eshtah parteedoo*
The flash isn't working	O flash não funciona *oo flash now foonsyona*

Processing and prints

I'd like to have this film developed/printed	Eu queria mandar revelar/ reproduzir este rolo *eyoo kerria mandar revelar/ reprodoozeer esht rolloo*
I'd like...prints from each negative	Eu queria...cópias de cada negativo *eyoo kerria...copeeash duh cadda negateevoo*
I'd like glossy/mat prints	Eu queria cópias brilhantes/mates *eyoo kerria copeeash breelyantesh/matsh*
I'd like 6x9 prints	Eu queria cópias seis por nove *eyoo kerria copeeash saysh poor nov*
I'd like to order these photos	Eu queria encomendar estas fotos *eyoo kerria aincoomendar eshtash fotoosh*
I'd like to have this photo enlarged	Eu queria mandar ampliar esta foto *eyoo kerria mandar ampliar eshta fotoo*
How much is processing?	Quanto custa a revelação? *cuarntoo cooshta a revellasow?*
How much is printing?	Quanto custa a reprodução? *cuarntoo cooshta a reprodoosow?*
How much is it to re-order?	Quanto custa mandar fazer mais cópias? *cuarntoo cooshta mandar fazair mysh copeeash?*
How much is an enlargement?	Quanto custa uma ampliação? *cuarntoo cooshta ooma ampleeasow*
When will they be ready?	Quando estão prontas? *cuarndoo eshtow prontash?*

10.5 At the hairdresser's

Do I have to make an appointment?	Tenho de marcar hora? *tenyoo duh marcar ora?*
Can I come in straight away?	Pode atender-me já? *pod atendair muh jah?*
How long will I have to wait?	Quanto tempo tenho de esperar? *quarntoo tempoo tenyoo duh eshpairar?*
I'd like a hairwash/haircut	Eu queria lavar/cortar o meu cabelo *eyoo kerria lavar/cortar oo mayoo cabayloo*
I'd like a shampoo for oily/dry hair	Eu queria um champô para cabelo gorduroso/seco *eyoo kerria oom shampoh parra cabayloo gordooroso/saycoo*
– an anti-dandruff shampoo	Eu queria um champô contra a caspa *eyoo kerria oom shampoh contra a cashpa*
– a shampoo for permed/coloured hair	Eu queria um champô para cabelo com permanente/pintado *eyoo kerria oom shampoh parra cabayloo com permanent/peentardoo*
– a colour rinse shampoo	Eu queria um champô com cor *eyoo kerria oom shampoh com cor*
– a shampoo with conditioner	Eu queria um champô com condicionador *eyoo kerria oom shampoh com condicionardoor*
– highlights	Eu queria madeixas *eyoo kerria madayshash*
Do you have a colour chart, please?	Tem um catálogo com as cores? *taim oom cataloggoo com ash coresh?*
I want to keep it the same colour	Eu queria manter a mesma cor *eyoo kerria mantair a mejma cor*
I'd like my hair darker/lighter	Eu queria o cabelo mais escuro/claro *eyoo kerria oo cabayloo maiz eshcooroo/claroo*
I'd like/I don't want hairspray	Quero (não quero) laca no meu cabelo *cairoo (now cairoo) larca noo mayoo cabayloo*
– gel	Quero (não quero) gel *cairoo (now cairoo) jel*
– mousse	Quero (não quero) mousse *cairoo (now cairoo) mousse*
I'd like a short fringe	Queria a franja curta *kerria a franja coorta*
Not too short at the back	Atrás não queria demasiado curto *atraj now kerria demaziardoo coortoo*
Not too long here	Aqui não quero muito comprido *akee now cairoo mweentoo coompreedoo*
I'd like (just a few) curls	Quero (não muitos) caracóis *cairoo (now mueentoosh) carracoysh*
It needs a little/a lot taken off	Corte um pouco/bastante *cort oom poecoo/bashtant*
I want a completely different style	Queria um modelo totalmente diferente *kerria oom moodeloo tootalment deeferent*
I'd like it as...	Queria o meu cabelo como... *kerria oo mayoo cabayloo comoo...*

– that lady's	Queria o meu cabelo como o daquela senhora *kerria oo may cabayloo comoo oo dakella senyora*
– in this photo	Queria o meu cabelo como o desta foto *kerria oo mayoo cabayloo comoo oo desta fotoo*
Could you put the drier up/down a bit?	Podia pôr o secador mais forte/fraco? *poodia poor oo secadoor maish fort/frarcoo?*
I'd like a facial	Queria uma máscara para o rosto *kerria ooma mashcara parra oo roshtoo*
– a manicure	Queria que me fizesse uma manicure *kerria kuh me feezess ooma manicure*
– a massage	Queria uma massagem *kerria ooma massarjaim*
Could you trim my fringe?	Podia aparar-me a franja? *poodia aparar muh a franja?*
– my beard?	Podia aparar-me a barba? *poodia aparar muh a barba?*
– my moustache?	Podia aparar-me o bigode? *poodia aparar muh oo beegod?*
I'd like a shave, please	A barba, se faz favor *a barba, se faj favvor*
I'd like a wet shave	Queria a barba feita com navalha *kerria a barba fayta com navaly*

Como deseja o cabelo cortado?	How do you want it cut?
Que modelo deseja?	What style did you have in mind?
Que cor deseja?	What colour do you want it?
Esta temperatura está boa?	Is the temperature all right for you?
Deseja alguma coisa para ler?	Would you like something to read?
Deseja beber alguma coisa?	Would you like a drink?
Está bem assim?	Is this what you had in mind?

At the Tourist Information Centre

11

11 At the Tourist Information Centre

11.1 Places of interest

Where's the Tourist Information Centre?	Onde é o posto de turismo? *ond eh oo poshtoo duh tooreeshmoo?*
Do you have a city map?	Tem uma planta da cidade? *taim ooma planta dah sidarde?*
Where is the museum?	Onde é o museu? *ond eh oo moozayoo?*
Where can I find a church?	Onde há uma igreja? *ond ah ooma eegrayja?*
Could you give me some information about...?	Podia dar-me alguma informação sobre...? *poodia dar muh algooma eenformasow sobre...?*
How much do we have to pay you?	Quanto é que temos de lhe pagar? *cuarntoo eh kuh taymoosh duh lya pagar?*
What are the main places of interest?	Quais são as atrações mais importantes? *quysh sow ash atrasoynsh maiz eemportantesh?*
Could you point them out on the map?	Podia indicá-las no mapa? *poodia eendeecar lash noo marpa?*
What do you recommend?	O que é que nos aconselha? *oo kuh eh kuh nooz aconselya?*
We'll be here for a few hours	Ficamos aqui umas horas *feecarmoos akee oomash orash*
– a day	Ficamos aqui um dia *feecarmoos akee oom deah*
– a week	Ficamos aqui uma semana *feecarmoos akee ooma semarna*
We're interested in...	Estamos interessados em... *eshtarmoosh eenteressardoosh aim...*
Is there a scenic walk around the city?	Podemos fazer um passeio turístico pela cidade? *poodaymoosh fazair oom passayoo tooreeshteecoo pella sidarde?*
How long does it take?	Quanto tempo demora? *cuarntoo tempoo demoora?*
Where does it start/end?	Onde começa/acaba? *ond comessa/acarba?*
Are there any boat cruises here?	Há aqui barcos de excursão? *ah akee barcoosh duh eshcoorsow?*
Where can we board?	Onde é que podemos embarcar? *ond eh kuh poodaymoosh embarcar?*
Are there any bus tours?	Há excursões de autocarro? *ah eshcoorsoynsh duh outoocahroo?*
Where do we get on?	Onde é que podemos entrar? *ond eh kuh poodaymoosh entrar?*
Is there a guide who speaks English?	Há um guia que fale inglês? *ah oom gueeah kuh fal eenglayj?*

What trips can we take around the area?	Que passeios podemos dar nos arredores?	*kay passayoosh poodaymoosh dar nooz arredooresh?*
Are there any excursions?	Há excursões?	*ah eshcoorsoynsh?*
Where do they go to?	Para onde vão as excursões?	*parra ond vow az eshcoorsoynsh?*
We'd like to go to...	Nós queremos ir a...	*nosh kerraymooz eer ah...*
How long is the excursion?	Quanto tempo demora a excursão?	*cuarntoo tempoo demoora ah eshcoorsow?*
How long do we stay in...?	Quanto tempo ficamos em...?	*cuarntoo tempoo feecarmoosh aim...?*
Are there any guided tours?	Há visitas guiadas?	*ah veezeetash gueeardash?*
How much free time will we have there?	Quanto tempo temos só para nós?	*cuarntoo tempoo taymoosh soh parra noj?*
We want to go hiking	Queriamos fazer uma caminhada	*kerriamoosh fazair ooma cameenyarda*
Can we hire a guide?	Podemos contratar um guia?	*poodaymoosh contratar oom gueeah?*
Can I book mountain huts?	Posso reservar abrigos?	*possoo resairvar abreegoosh?*
What time does... open/close?	A que horas abre/fecha...?	*ah kay orash abre/faysha...?*
What days is...open/closed?	Em que dias está aberto/fechado...?	*aim kuh deeash eshtah abairtoo/fechardoo...?*
What's the admission price?	Quanto custa a entrada?	*cuarntoo cooshta ah entrarda?*
Is there a group discount?	Há desconto para grupos?	*ah deshcontoo parra groopoosh?*
Is there a child discount?	Há desconto para crianças?	*ah deshcontoo parra creeansash?*
Is there a discount for pensioners?	Há desconto para reformados?	*ah deshcontoo parra reformardoosh?*
Can I take (flash) photos/can I film here?	Posso aqui fotografar (com flash)/filmar?	*possoo akee fotografar (com flash)/feelmar?*
Do you have any postcards of...?	Vende postais com...?	*vend pooshtysh com...?*
Do you have an English...?	Tem um/uma...em inglês?	*taim oom/ooma...aim eenglayj?*
– catalogue?	Tem um catálogo em inglês?	*taim oom catalogoo aim eenglayj?*
– programme?	Tem um programa em inglês?	*taim oom proograrma aim eenglayj?*
– brochure?	Tem um folheto em inglês?	*taim oom foolyetoo aim eenglayj?*

11.2 Going out

- **There are far fewer cinemas in Portugal** than in the UK. Usherettes will normally expect a small tip. Most films shown are in English with Portuguese subtitles, which is very convenient. Sometimes the name given to the film in Portuguese is completely different from its original. Details of theatre and cinema programmes are to be found in the national newspapers, especially in the Friday editions. Showings are generally much later than in the UK and theatre performances are often subject to considerable delay.

Do you have this week's/month's entertainment guide?	Tem o jornal de espectáculos desta semana/deste mês? *taim oo jornarl di eshpetarcooloosh deshta semarna/deshta mayge?*
What's on tonight?	O que é que há para fazer esta noite? *oo kee eh kuh ah parra fazzair eshta noyt?*
We want to go to...	Queríamos ir a... *kerriamoosh eer ah...*
Which films are showing?	Que filmes estão a passar? *kuh feelmesh eshtow ah passar?*
What sort of film is it?	Que género de filme é? *kuh jenroo duh feelm eh?*
It's suitable for all ages	É para todas as idades *eh parra toedaz az eedardesh*
It's only for people above 12/16 years	É só para pessoas acima dos 12/16 anos *eh sooh parra pessowash aseema dooz 12/16 arnoosh*
It's the original version	É a versão original *eh ah versow ooreegeenarl*
It's subtitled	É com legendas *eh com lejendash*
It's dubbed	É dobrado *eh doobrardoo*
Is it a continuous showing?	São sessões contínuas? *sow sessoynsh conteenooash?*
What's on at...?	Qual é o programa do...? *quarl eh oo proograrma doo...?*
– the theatre?	Qual é o programa do teatro? *quarl eh oo proograrma doo teeartroo?*
– the concert hall?	Qual é o programa de concertos? *quarl eh oo proograrma duh consairtoosh?*
– the opera?	Qual é o programa da ópera? *quarl eh oo proograrma dah ohpairah?*
Where can I find a good disco around here?	Onde é que há uma boa discoteca aqui? *ond eh kuh ha ooma boa deeshcooteca akee?*
Does one have to be a member?	É necessário ser membro? *eh necessaryoo sair membroo?*
Where can I find a good nightclub around here?	Onde é que há um bom clube nocturno aqui? *ond eh kuh ah oom bom cloob notoornoo akee?*
Is it evening wear only?	É obrigatório traje de cerimónia? *eh obreegatoryoo trarj duh cerimonnia?*

Should I/we dress up?	É aconselhável traje a preceito? *eh aconselyarvel trarj ah presaytoo?*
What time does the show start?	A que horas começa o show? *ah kay orash coomessa oo show?*
When's the next soccer match?	Quando é o próximo jogo de futebol? *cuarndoo eh oo prosseemoo jogoo duh footebol?*
Who's playing?	Quem é que vai jogar? *caim eh kuh vy joogar?*
I'd like an escort for tonight. Could you arrange that for me?	Queria ter um/uma acompanhante para hoje a noite. Pode tratar-me disto? *kerria tair oom/ooma acompanyant parra oarje a noyt. pod tratar muh deeshtoo?*

11.3 Booking tickets

We'd like to book...	Queríamos reservar... *kerriamoosh rezairvar...*
– seats in the stalls	Queríamos reservar...lugares na plateia *kerriamoosh rezairvar...loogaresh na plataya*
– seats on the balcony	Queríamos reservar...lugares no balcão *kerriamoosh rezairvar...loogaresh noo balcow*
– a table at the front	Queríamos reservar uma mesa à frente *kerriamoosh rezairvar ooma mayza ah frent*
– seats in the centre	Queríamos reservar...lugares a meio *kerriamoosh rezairvar...loogaresh ah mayoo*
– seats at the back	Queríamos reservar...lugares atrás *kerriamoosh rezairvar...loogaresh atraj*
Could I book...seats for the...o'clock performance?	Posso reservar...lugares para a sessão das...? *possoo resairvar...loogaresh parra a sessow dash...?*
Are there any tickets left for tonight?	Ainda há bilhetes para esta noite? *ayeenda ah beelyetsch parra eshta noyt?*
How much is a ticket?	Quanto custa um bilhete? *cuarntoo cooshta oom beelyet?*
When can I pick the tickets up?	Quando é que posso levantar os bilhetes? *cuarndoo eh kuh possoo levantaroosh beelyetsch?*
I've got a reservation	Reservei *resairvay*
My name's...	O meu nome é... *oo mayoo nom eh...*

Para que sessão é que deseja reservar?	Which performance do you want to book for?
Onde é que deseja se sentar?	Where would you like to sit?
Está esgotado	Everything's sold out
Só há lugares de pé	We've only got standing spaces left
Só há lugares no balcão	We've only got balcony seats left
Só há lugares na geral	We've only got seats left in the gallery
Só há lugares na plateia	We've only got stalls seats left
Só há lugares à frente	We've only got seats left at the front
Só há lugares atrás	We've only got seats left at the back
Quantos lugares deseja?	How many seats would you like?
Tem de levantar os bilhetes antes das...horas	You'll have to pick up the tickets before...o'clock
Posso ver os seus bilhetes?	Tickets, please
Este é o seu lugar	This is your seat
Estâo em lugares errados	You're in the wrong seats

12

Sports

12 Sports

12.1 Sporting questions

Where can we...around here?	Onde é que podemos...aqui? *ond eh kuh poodaymooz...akee?*
Is there a...nearby?	Há um...perto daqui? *ah oom...pairtoo dackee?*
Can I hire a...here?	Posso alugar um/uma...aqui? *possoo aloogar oom/ooma...akee?*
Can I take...lessons?	Posso ter lições de...? *possoo tair leesoynsh duh...?*
How much is it per hour/per day/a turn?	Quanto custa por hora/dia/vez? *cuarntoo cooshta por ora/deeah/vaij?*
Do I need a permit?	É preciso uma licença? *eh preseezoo ooma leesensa?*
Where can I get the permit?	Onde é que posso tirar a licença? *ond eh kuh possoo teerar a leesensa?*

12.2 By the waterfront

Is it a long way (by foot) to the sea?	É muito longe (a pé) daqui ao mar? *eh mueentoo lonj (ah peh) dakee ow mar?*
Is there...nearby?	Há um/uma...perto daqui? *ah akee oom/ooma...pairtoo dackee?*
– an outdoor/indoor/public swimming pool nearby?	Há uma piscina perto daqui? *ah ooma peeshseena pairtoo dackee?*
– a sandy beach nearby?	Há aqui uma praia de areia perto? *ah akee ooma prya di araya pairtoo?*
– a nudist beach nearby?	Há uma praia de naturistas perto daqui? *ah ooma prya duh natooreeshtash pairtoo dackee?*
– a quay nearby?	Há um cais perto daqui? *ah oom kysh pairtoo dackee?*
Are there any rocks here?	Há rochas aqui? *ah roshash akee?*
When's high/low tide?	Quando é a maré cheia/a maré vazia? *cuarndoo eh a maray shaya/a maray vazeeah?*
What's the water temperature?	Qual é a temperatura da água? *cuarl eh a temperatoora da agwar?*
Is it (very) deep here?	Aqui é (muito) fundo? *akee eh mweentoo foondoo?*
Can I reach the ground here?	Aqui tenho pé? *akee tenyoo peh?*
Is it safe to swim here?	É seguro nadar aqui (para as crianças)? *eh segooroo nadar akee (parra ash creansash)?*
Are there any currents?	Há correntes? *ah coorentesh?*
Are there any rapids/waterfalls in this river?	Este rio tem rápidos/cataratas? *esht reeoo taim rappeedoosh/cataratash?*

What does that flag/ buoy mean?	O que significa aquela bandeira/bóia? *oo kuh signeefeeca akela bandayra/boya?*
Is there a life guard on duty here?	Há aqui um salva-vidas? *ah akee oom salva-veedash?*
Are dogs allowed here?	São permitidos cães aqui? *sow permeeteedoosh caynz akee?*
Is camping on the beach allowed?	Pode-se acampar aqui na praia? *pod suh acampar akee na prya?*
Is it permitted to build a fire here?	Pode-se fazer uma fogueira aqui? *pod suh fazair ooma foogayra akee?*

Perigo	É proibido pescar	É proibido nadar
Danger	No fishing	No swimming
É permitido pescar	É proibido fazer surf	Só com licença
Fishing allowed	No surfing	Permits only

13 Sickness

13

Sickness

13.1 Call (fetch) the doctor

Could you call/fetch a doctor quickly, please?	Podia chamar/ir buscar um médico depressa, se faz favor? *poodia shamar/eer booshcar oom maydeecoo, suh faj favvor?*
When does the doctor have surgery?	Quando é a consulta do médico? *cuarndoo eh a consoolta doo meydeecoo?*
When can the doctor come?	Quando é que o médico pode vir? *cuarndoo eh kuh oo meydeecoo pod veer?*
I'd like to make an appointment to see the doctor	Podia marcar-me uma consulta no médico? *poodia marcar muh ooma consoolta noo meydeecoo?*
I've got an appointment to see the doctor at...	Tenho uma consulta no médico às...horas *tenyoo ooma consoolta noo meydeecoo az...orash*
Which doctor/chemist has night/weekend duty?	Que médico/farmácia tem serviço nocturno/de fim de semana? *kuh meydeecoo/farmassia taim sairveesoo notoornoo/duh feem duh semarna?*

13.2 Patient's ailments

I don't feel well	Não me sinto bem *now muh seentoo baim*
I'm dizzy	Tenho tonturas *tenyoo tontoorash*
I feel ill	Sinto-me doente *seentoo muh dooent*
I feel sick	Sinto-me enjoado *seento muh enjooardoo*
I've got a cold	Sinto-me constipado *seento muh conshteepardoo*
It hurts here	Dói-me aqui *doy muh akee*
I've been throwing up	Vomitei *voomeetay*
I've got a headache	Tenho dor de cabeca *tenyoo door duh cabaysa*
I'm running a temperature of...degrees	Tenho...graus de febre *tenyoo...growsh duh febre*
I've been stung by a wasp	Fui picado por uma abelha *fwee peecardoo por ooma abelya*
I've been stung by an insect	Fui picado por um insecto *fwee picardoo por oom eensetoo*
I've been bitten by a dog	Fui mordido por um cão *fwee mordeedoo por oom cow*
I've been stung by a jellyfish	Fui mordido por uma alforreca *fwee mordeedoo por ooma alfooreka*
I've been bitten by a snake	Fui mordido por uma cobra *fwee mordeedoo por ooma cobbra*

I've been bitten by an animal	Fui mordido por um bicho *fwee mordeedoo por oom beeshoo*
I've cut myself	Cortei-me *cortay muh*
I've burned myself	Queimei-me *kaymay muh*
I've grazed myself	Fiz um arranhão *feez oom aranyow*
I've had a fall	Caí *ky*
I've sprained my ankle	Torci o tornozelo *torsee oo toornnzeloo*
I've come for a morning-after pill	Venho pedir uma pílula `morning-after' *venyoo pedeer ooma peeloola 'morning-after'*

13.3 The consultation

O que tem?	What seems to be the problem?
Há quanto tempo sofre disto?	How long have you had these symptoms?
Já teve isto antes?	Have you had this trouble before?
Que febre tem?	How high is your temperature?
Podia despir-se, se faz favor?	Get undressed, please
Podia despir-se da cintura para cima?	Strip to the waist
Pode despir-se ali	You can undress there
Puxe a manga esquerda/direita para cima?	Roll up your left/right sleeve
Deite-se aqui	Lie down here
Isto faz-lhe doer?	Does this hurt?
Respire fundo	Breathe deeply
Abra a boca	Open your mouth

Patient's medical history

I'm a diabetic	Sofro de diabetes *sofroo duh deeabetsh*
I have a heart condition	Sofro do coração *sofroo doo coorasow*
I have asthma	Sofro de asma *sofroo di ajma*
I'm allergic to...	Sou alérgico a... *soe alergeeco ah...*
I'm...months pregnant	Estou grávida de...meses *eshtoe graveeda duh...meyzesh*
I'm on a diet	Estou de dieta *eshtoe duh deeayta*
I'm on medication/the pill	Tomo medicamentos/a pílula *tomoo medeecamentoosh/a peeloola*

I've had a heart attack once before	Já tive outro ataque cardíaco *jah teev ohtroo atak cardeeacoo*
I've had a...operation	Fui operado de... *fwee operardoo duh...*
I've been ill recently	Estive doente recentemente *eshteev dooent recentement*
I've got an ulcer	Tenho uma úlcera *tenyoo ooma oolsera*
I've got my period	Estou com a menstruação *eshtoe com a menshtrooasow*

The diagnosis

Is it contagious?	É contagioso? *eh contajiozoo?*
How long do I have to stay...?	Quanto tempo tenho de ficar...? *cuarntoo tempoo tenyoo duh feecar...?*
– in bed	Quanto tempo tenho de ficar de cama? *cuarntoo tempoo tenyoo duh feecar duh camma?*
– in hospital	Quanto tempo tenho de ficar no hospital? *cuarntoo tempoo tenyoo duh feecar noo oshpeetal?*

É alérgico a qualquer coisa?	Do you have any allergies?
Toma medicamentos?	Are you on any medication?
Faz qualquer dieta?	Are you on any sort of diet?
Está grávida?	Are you pregnant?
Está vacinado contra o tétano?	Have you had a tetanus vaccination?
Não é nada de grave	It's nothing serious
Partiu o/a...	You've broken your...
Magoou o/a...	You've bruised your...
Estalou o/a...	You've split your...
Tem uma inflamacão	You've got an inflammation
Tem uma apendicite	You've got appendicitis
Tem uma bronquite	You've got bronchitis
Tem uma doença venérea	You've got a venereal disease
Tem uma gripe	You've got the flu
Teve um ataque cardíaco	You've had a heart attack
Tem uma infecção (provocada por um vírus/uma bactéria)	You've got an infection (viral/bacteria)
Tem uma infecção pulmonar	You've got pneumonia
Tem uma úlcera	You've got an ulcer
Distendeu um músculo	You've pulled a muscle
Tem uma infecção na vagina	You've got a vaginal infection
Tem uma intoxicação de alimentos	You've got food poisoning

Apanhou uma insolação	You've got sunstroke
É alérgico a...	You're allergic to...
Está grávida	You're pregnant
Tem de fazer análises ao sangue/à urina/às fezes	You'll need to have your blood/urine/stools tested
Tem de levar pontos	It needs stitching
Tem de ir a um especialista/para o hospital	I'm referring you to a specialist/sending you to hospital
Tem de tirar radiografias	You'll need to have some x-rays taken
Pode aguardar ainda na sala de espera, se faz favor?	Could you wait in the waiting room, please?
Tem de ser operado	You'll need an operation

Do I have to go on a special diet?	Tenho de fazer alguma dieta? *tenyoo duh fazair algooma diayta?*
Am I allowed to travel?	Posso viajar? *possoo veajar?*
Can I make a new appointment?	Posso marcar outra consulta? *possoo marcar ohtra conssoolta?*
When do I have to come back?	Quando é que tenho de voltar? *cuarndoo eh kuh tenyoo duh voltar?*
I'll come back tomorrow	Volto amanhã *voltoo armanyar*

Volte amanhã/daqui a...dias	Come back tomorrow/in...days' time

13.4 Medication and prescriptions

How do I take this medicine?	Como é que tenho de tomar este medicamento? *coemoo eh kuh tenyoo duh toomar esht medeecamentoo?*
How many capsules/ drops/injections/ spoonfuls/tablets each time?	Quantas cápsulas/gotas/injecções/ colheres/comprimidos de uma vez? *cuarntash capsoolash/gottash, eenjecsoynsh/coolyairesh/compreemeedosh di ooma vej?*
How many times a day?	Quantas vezes por dia? *cuarntash vayzesh por deeah?*
I've forgotten my medication. At home I take...	Esqueci-me dos meus medicamentos. Costumo tomar... *eshkessee muh doosh mayoosh meydeecamentoosh. coshtoomoo toomar...*
Could you make out a prescription for me?	Podia passar-me uma receita? *poodia passar muh ooma ressayta?*

Receito-lhe um antibiótico/xarope/ sedativo/analgésico	I'm prescribing antibiotics/a mixture/a tranquillizer/pain killers
Tem de descansar	You need to rest
Tem de ficar dentro de casa	Stay indoors
Tem de ficar na cama	Stay in bed

antes das refeições
before meals
cápsulas
capsules
dissolver em água
dissolve in water
comprimidos
tablets
colheres (de sopa/de chá)
spoonfuls (tablespoons/ teaspoons)

durante...dias
for...days
engolir inteiro
swallow whole
esfregar
rub on
gotas
drops
injecções
injections
pomada
ointment
...vezes por dia
...times a day

só para uso externo
only for external use
terminar a cura
finish the prescription
tomar
take
este medicamento pode influenciar a condução
this medication impairs your driving

13.5 At the dentist's

Do you know a good dentist?	Conhece um bom dentista? *coonyess oom bom denteeshta?*
Could you make a dentist's appointment for me? It's urgent	Podia marcar-me uma consulta no dentista? É urgente *poodia marcar muh ooma consoolta noo denteeshta? Eh oorgent*
Can I come in today, please?	Podia ser ainda hoje? *poodia sair ayeenda oarje?*
I have (terrible) toothache	Tenho (imensa) dor de dentes *tenyoo (eemensa) door duh dentesh*
Could you prescribe/ give me a painkiller?	Podia receitar-me um analgésico? *poodia ressaytar muh oom analjezzeecoo?*
One of my teeth has cracked	Partiu-se um dos meus dentes *partyoo suh oom doosh mayoosh dentesh*
My filling's come out	O chumbo do dente caiu *oo choomboo doo dent cayoo*
I've got a cracked crown	Partiu-se a coroa *partyoo suh ah coroah*
I'd like/I don't want a local anaesthetic	Gostava/não gostava de anestesia local *goshtarv/now goshtarv duh aneshtezia loocal*
Can you do a makeshift repair job?	Podia fazer um arranjo provisório? *poodia fazair oom arranjoo prooveesoryoo?*
I don't want this tooth pulled	Não quero que arranque este dente *now cairoo kuh arrank esht dent*

My dentures are broken. Can you fix them?	A minha dentadura partiu-se. Podia arranjá-la? *a meenya dentadoora partyoo suh. Poodia arranjar la?*

Que dente lhe dói?	Which tooth hurts?
Tem um abcesso	You've got an abscess
Tem de fazer um tratamento ao nervo	I'll have to do a root canal
Vou fazer uma anestesia local	I'm giving you a local anaesthetic
Tenho de chumbar/tirar/limar este dente	I'll have to fill/pull/file this tooth
Tenho de brocar	I'll have to drill
Abra a boca	Open your mouth
Feche a boca	Close your mouth
Bochechar	Rinse
Ainda sente dores?	Does it hurt still?

14 In trouble

14 In trouble

14.1 Asking for help

Help!	**Socorro!** *socooroo!*
Fire!	**Fogo!** *foegoo!*
Police!	**Polícia!** *pooleecia!*
Quick!	**Depressa!** *depressa!*
Danger!	**Perigo!** *pereegoo!*
Watch out!	**Atenção!** *atensow*
Stop!	**Páre!** *parah!*
Be careful!	**Cuidado!** *cweedardoo*
Don't!	**Não faça isso!** *now fassa eessoo!*
Let go!	**Largar!** *largar!*
Stop that thief!	**Apanhe o ladrão!** *apanya oo ladrow!*
Could you help me, please?	**Podia ajudar-me?** *poodia ajoodar muh?*
Where's the police station/emergency exit/fire escape?	**Onde é a polícia/a saída de emergência/a escada de incêndios?** *ond eh a pooleecia/a sayeeda di emerjencia/a eshcarda di eencendyoosh?*
Where's the nearest fire extinguisher?	**Onde está o extintor?** *ond eshtah oo eshteentor?*
Call the fire brigade!	**Chame os bombeiros!** *shamma oosh bombayroosh!*
Call the police!	**Telefone à polícia** *telefon ah pooleecia!*
Call an ambulance!	**Chame uma ambulância** *shamma ooma amboolancia*
Where's the nearest phone?	**Onde é o telefone?** *ond eh oo telefon?*
Could I use your phone?	**Posso usar o seu telefone?** *possoo oozar oo sayoo telefon?*
What's the emergency number?	**Qual é o número de urgência?** *cuarl eh oo noomeroo duh oorjensia?*
What's the number for the police?	**Qual é o número da polícia?** *cuarl eh oo noomeroo da pooleecia?*

14.2 Loss

I've lost my purse/wallet	**Perdi o meu porta-moedas/a minha carteira** *pairdee oo mayoo porta mooaydash/a meenya cartayra*
I lost my...yesterday	**Ontem esqueci-me do meu/da minha...** *ontaim eshkecee muh doo mayoo/da meenya...*
I left my...here	**Deixei aqui o meu/a minha...** *dayshay akee oo mayoo/a meenya...*
Did you find my...?	**Encontrou o meu/a minha...?** *encontroe oo mayoo/a meenya...?*
It was right here	**Estava aqui** *eshtarva akee*
It's quite valuable	**É bastante valioso** *eh bashtant valiozoo*
Where's the lost property office?	**Onde é a secção de perdidos e achados?** *ond eh a seksow duh pairdeedoos e achardoosh?*

14.3 Accidents

There's been an accident	**Houve um acidente** *ohve oom asseedent*
Someone's fallen into the water	**Caiu uma pessoa na água** *cayoo ooma pessoa nah agwa*
There's a fire	**Há fogo** *ha foegoo*
Is anyone hurt?	**Alguém está ferido?** *algaim eshtah fereedoo?*
No one's been injured	**Não há feridos** *now ah fereedoosh*
Some people have been injured	**Há alguns feridos** *ah algoons fereedoosh*
There's still someone in the car/train	**Ainda há uma pessoa no carro/comboio** *ayeenda hah ooma pessoa noo cahroo/comboyoo*
It's not too bad. Don't worry	**Não é nada. Não se preocupe** *now eh narda. Now suh preeocoop*
Don't touch anything	**Não mexa em nada** *now mesha aim narda*
I want to talk to the police first	**Queria falar primeiro com a polícia** *kerria falar preemayroo com a pooleecia*
I want to take a photo first	**Primeiro quero tirar uma fotografia** *preemayroo cairoo teerar ooma fotografeea*
Here's my name and address	**Tem aqui o meu nome e morada** *taim akee oo mayoo nom ee moorarda*
Could I have your name and address?	**Podia dar-me o seu nome e morada?** *poodia dar muh oo sayoo nom e moorarda?*
Could I see some identification/your insurance papers?	**Posso ver os seus documentos de identificação/o seu seguro?** *possoo vair oosh sayoosh docoomentoosh di eedentifeecasow/oo sayoo segooroo?*

Will you act as a witness?	Quer ser testemunha? *care sair teshtemoonya?*
I need to know the details for the insurance	Tenho de saber os dados para o seguro *tenyoo duh sabbair oosh dardoosh parra oo segooroo*
Are you insured?	Tem um seguro? *taim oom segooroo?*
Third party or comprehensive?	Contra terceiros ou contra todos os riscos? *contra tairsayroosh o contra toedoos oosh reeshcoosh?*
Could you sign here, please?	Podia assinar aqui? *poodia asseenar akee?*

14.4 Theft

I've been robbed	Fui roubado *fwee roobardoo*
My...has been stolen	Roubaram-me o meu/a minha... *roobaram muh oo mayoo/a meenya...*
My car's been broken into	Assaltaram-me o carro *assalltaram muh oo cahroo*

14.5 Missing person

I've lost my child/ grandmother	Perdi o meu filho (a minha filha)/a minha avó *pairdee oo mayoo feelyoo (a meenya feelya)/a meenya avoh*
Could you help me find him/her?	Podia ajudar-me a procurar? *poodia ajoodar muh a procoorar?*
Have you seen a small child?	Viu uma criança pequena? *veeoo ooma creeansa peekayna?*
He's/she's...years old	Ele/ela tem...anos *el/alla taim...arnoosh*
He's/she's got short/long/blond/red/ brown/black/grey/ straight/curly/frizzy hair	Ele/ela tem cabelo curto/comprido/louro/ ruivo/castanho/preto/grisalho/liso/ encaracolado/frizado *el/ella taim cabayloo coortoo/rooeevoo/cashtanyoo/ praytoo/greesalyoo/leezoo/ aincarracoolardoo/freezardoo*
in a ponytail	tem rabo de cavalo *taim rarboo duh cavarloo*
in plaits	tem tranças *taim transash*
in a bun	tem um carrapito *taim oom carrapeetoo*
He's/she's got blue/brown/green eyes	Os olhos são azuis/castanhos/verdes *ooz olyoosh sow azweesh/castanyoosh/vairdsh*
He's wearing swimming trunks/mountaineering boots	Tem uns calções de banho vestidos/uns sapatos de alpinismo calçados *taim unsh calsoynsh de bahnyoo veshteedoosh/unsh sapartoosh di alpeeneejmoo calsardoosh*

with/without glasses/ a bag	com/sem óculos/saco *com/saim occooloosh/sarcoo*
tall/short	grande/pequeno *grand/peekaynoo*
This is a photo of him/her	Esta fotografia é dele/dela *eshta fotoografeea eh del/della*
He/she must be lost	Com certeza ele/ela se perdeu *com sairtayza el/ella suh pairdayoo*

14.6 The police

An arrest

I don't speak Portuguese	Não falo português *now faloo poortoogayj*
I didn't see that sign	Não vi aquele sinal *now vee akel seenal*
I don't understand what it says	Não compreendo o que significa *now comprayendoo oo kuh seegneefeeca*
I was only doing... kilometres an hour	Só vinha a...km por hora *soh veenya a...km poor ora*
I'll have my car checked	Vou levar o meu carro à oficina *voe levvar oo mayoo cahro ah offeeseena*
I was blinded by oncoming lights	Fiquei encadeado pelos faróis em sentido contrário *feekay encaddeardoo peloosh faroysh aim senteedoo contraryoo*

Os seus documentos, se faz favor	Your registration papers, please
Excedeu a velocidade máxima	You were speeding
Está mal estacionado	You're not allowed to park here
Não pôs dinheiro no parquímetro	You haven't put money in the meter
As luzes não funcionam	Your lights aren't working
É uma multa de...escudos	That's a...escudos fine
Quer pagar agora?	Do you want to pay on the spot?
Tem de pagar agora	You'll have to pay on the spot

At the police station

I want to report a collision/missing person/rape	Venho declarar uma colisão/um desaparecimento/uma violação *venyoo declarar ooma cooleesow/oom dezaparessimentoo/ooma veeoolasow*
Could you make out a report, please?	Podia fazer um relatório, se faz favor? *poodia fazair oom relatoryoo, suh faj favvor?*
Could I have a copy for the insurance?	Posso levar uma cópia para o seguro? *possoo levvar ooma copia parra oo segooroo?*

I've lost everything — **Perdi tudo**
pairdee toodoo

I've no money at all. I'm desperate — **Não tenho dinheiro nenhum. Estou desesperado**
now tenyoo deenyayroo nenyoom. eshtoe deseshperardoo

Can you lend me some money? — **Pode emprestar-me algum dinheiro?**
poodia empreshtar muh algoom deenyayroo?

I'd like an interpreter — **Queria um intérprete**
kerria oom eentairpret

Onde é que aconteceu?	Where did it happen?
O que é que perdeu?	What's missing?
O que é que foi roubado?	What's been taken?
Tem os seus documentos de identificação?	Do you have some identification?
A que horas aconteceu?	What time did it happen?
Quem são os outros?	Who are the others?
Há testemunhas?	Are there any witnesses?
Preencha isto, se faz favor	Fill this out, please
Assinar aqui, se faz favor	Sign here, please
Quer um intérprete?	Do you want an interpreter?

I'm innocent — **Estou inocente**
eshtoe eenoosent

I don't know anything about it — **Não sei nada**
now say narda

I want to speak to someone from the British consulate — **Queria falar com alguém do Consulado Britânico**
kerria falar com algaim doo consoolardoo breetaneecoo

I want to speak to someone from the British embassy — **Queria falar com alguém da Embaixada Britânica**
kerria falar com algaim da embysharda breetaneeca

I want a lawyer who speaks English — **Queria um advogado que fale inglês**
kerria oom advoogardoo kuh fal eenglayj

15

Word list

Word list English - Portuguese

● **This word list** is meant to supplement previous chapters. In a number of cases, words not contained in this list can be found elsewhere in this book, namely alongside the diagrams of the car, the bicycle and the tent. Many food terms can be found in the Portuguese-English list in 4.7

A

about	acerca de	*asserca duh*
above, up	em cima	*aim seema*
abroad	estrangeiro	*eshtranjayroo*
accident	acidente	*assident*
adder	víbora	*veebora*
addition	soma	*somma*
address	morada	*mooradah*
adhesive tape	fita cola	*feeta colla*
admission	entrada	*entrarda*
admission price	preço de entrada	*praysoo duh entrarda*
advice	conselho	*consellyoo*
after	depois	*depoysh*
afternoon	tarde	*tard*
aftershave	loção para a barba	*loosow parra ah barba*
again	novamente	*novvament*
against	contra	*contra*
age	idade	*eedarde*
Aids	Sida	*seeda*
air conditioning	ar condicionado	*ar condeesionardoo*
air mattress	colchão inflável	*colchow eenflarvel*
air sickness bag	saco para enjôo	*sarcoo parra ainjoh-oo*
aircraft	avião	*avviow*
airport	aeroporto	*airoopoortoo*
alarm	alarme	*alarm*
alarm clock	despertador	*deshpairtadoor*
alcohol	âlcool	*alcooolI*
allergic	alérgico	*alergeecoo*
alone	só	*soh*
always	sempre	*sempra*
ambulance	ambulância	*amboolancia*
amount	quantia, quantidade	*quarnteeah, quarnteedard*
amusement park	parque de diversôes	*park duh deevaisoynsh*
anaesthetize	anestesiar	*aneshteziar*
anchovy	anchovas	*anshovvash*
angry	zangado	*zangardoo*
animal	animal	*animarl*
ankle	tornozelo	*tornoozelloo*
answer	resposta	*reshposhta*
ant	formiga	*formeega*
antibiotics	antibióticos	*antibeeoteecoosh*
antifreeze	anticongelante	*anticongellant*
antique	antigo	*anteegoo*
antiques	antiguidades	*anteegweedardesh*
anus	ânus	*arnoosh*
apartment	apartamento	*apartamentoo*
aperitif	aperitivo	*aperiteevoo*
apologies	desculpas	*descoolpash*
apple	maçã	*massar*

apple juice	sumo de maçã	*soomoo duh massar*
apple pie	tarte de maçã	*tarte duh massar*
appointment	consulta	*consoolta*
apricot	alperce	*alpairce*
April	abril	*abreel*
architecture	arquitectura	*arkeetetoora*
area	arredores	*arredoresh*
arm	braço	*brarsoo*
arrange	combinar	*combeenar*
arrive	chegar	*sheggar*
arrow	seta	*setta*
art	arte	*art*
artery	artéria	*arterrya*
artichokes	alcachofras	*alcashoffrash*
article	artigo	*arteegoo*
artificial respiration	respiração artificial	*reshpeerasow arteefeecial*
ashtray	cinzeiro	*seenzayroo*
ask	perguntar	*pairgoontar*
ask	pedir	*pedeer*
asparagus	espargos	*eshpargoosh*
aspirin	aspirina	*ashpeereena*
assault	assalto	*assaltoo*
at home	em casa	*aim carza*
at last	afinal	*afeenal*
at night	à noite	*ah noyt*
at the back	atrás	*atraj*
at the front	à frente	*ah frent*
at the latest	no mais tardar	*noo mysh tardar*
aubergine	beringela	*berringella*
August	agosto	*agoshtoo*
automatic	automático	*owtoomateecoo*
automatically	automaticamente	*owtoomateecament*
autumn	outono	*ohtonoo*
awake	acordado	*acordardoo*
awning	toldo	*toldoo*

B

baby's bottle	biberão	*beeberow*
baby	bebé	*baybay*
baby car-seat	cadeira para bébé	*caddayra parra baybay*
baby food	comida para bébé	*comeeda parra baybay*
babysitter	babysitter	*baybeeseetair*
back	costas	*coshtash*
bacon	toucinho	*toosseenyoo*
bad	mau	*mow*
bad/off	estragado	*eshtragardoo*
bag (plastic)	saco (de plástico)	*sarcoo duh plashteecoo*
baker	padeiro	*paddayroo*
balcony (theatre)	balcão	*balcow*
balcony (of building)	varanda	*varanda*
ball	bola	*bolla*
ballet	ballet	*ballay*
ballpoint pen	esferográfica	*eshferoografeeca*
banana	banana	*bananna*
bandage	ligadura	*leegadoura*
bank (river)	margem	*marjaim*
bank	banco	*bancoo*

bar (café)	café	*cafay*
bar (drinks' cabinet)	bar	*bar*
barbecue	churrasco	*shoorashcoo*
bath	banho	*barnyoo*
bath foam	espuma de banho	*eshpooma duh barnyoo*
bath towel	toalha de banho	*tooalya duh barnyoo*
bath-tub	banheira	*banyayra*
bathing cap	touca de banho	*toeca duh barnyoo*
bathing suit	fato de banho	*fartoo duh barnyoo*
bathroom	casa de banho	*carza duh banyoo*
battery	pilha	*peelya*
battery	bateria	*batareeya*
be bored	aborrecer-se	*abooressair-suh*
be careful!	cuidado!	*cweedardoo*
be foggy	fazer nevoeiro	*fazzair nevooayroo*
be hungry	ter fome	*tair fom*
be in love with	estar namorado com	*eshtar namorardoo com*
be lost	perder-se	*pairdair-se*
be missing	faltar	*faltar*
be mistaken	enganar-se	*ainganar-suh*
beach	praia	*prya*
beautiful	lindo/belo	*leendoo/ bella*
beauty parlour	salão de beleza	*salow duh bellayza*
bed	cama	*camma*
bee	abelha	*abellya*
beef	carne de vaca	*carn duh varca*
beer	cerveja	*sairvayja*
beetroot	beterraba	*betterrarb*
begin	começar	*coomessar*
beginner	principiante	*preenseepeeant*
behind	atrás	*atraj*
belt	cinto	*seentoo*
beret	boina	*booeena*
berth	couchete	*cooshet*
better	melhor	*melyor*
bicarbonate of soda	bicarbonato de sódio	*beecarboonartoo duh sohdew*
bicycle	bicicleta	*beeseecletta*
bicycle pump	bomba de bicicleta	*bomba duh beeseecletta*
bicycle repair workshop	oficina de bicicletas	*offiseena duh beeseeclettash*
bikini	biquini	*bee-kee-nee*
bill	conta	*conta*
billiards, to play	jogar bilhar	*joogar beelyar*
birthday	aniversário	*anneevairsareeyoo*
birthday, to have a...	fazer anos	*fazzair arnoosh*
biscuit	biscoito	*beeshcoytoo*
bite	morder	*mordair*
bitter	amargo	*amargoo*
black	preto	*pretoo*
bland	insêpido	*eenseepeedoo*
blanket	cobertor	*coobertor*
bleach (hair)	pintar de louro	*peentar duh loroo*
bleeding nose	deitar sangue pelo nariz	*daytar sang peloo nareej*
blister	bolha	*bolya*
blond	louro	*loroo*

blood	sangue	*sang*
blood pressure	tensão arterial	*tensow arterrial*
blouse	blusa	*blooza*
blow dry	secar	*seccar*
blue	azul	*azool*
boat	barco	*barcoo*
body	corpo	*corpoo*
body milk	leite de beleza	*layt duh bellayza*
boiled	cozido	*coozeedoo*
boiled ham	fiambre	*feeambr*
bonbon	bombom	*bombom*
bone	osso	*ossoo*
bonnet	tampa do motor	*tampa doo motor*
book	livro	*leevroo*
book	reservar	*reservar*
booked	reservado	*reservardoo*
booking office	bilheteria	*beelyetareeah*
bookshop	livraria	*leevrareeah*
border	fronteira	*frontayra*
boring	monótono	*monotoonoo*
born/be born	nascido/nascer	*nashseedoo/nashayr*
borrow	pedir emprestado	*pedeer aimpreshtardoo*
botanical garden	jardim botânico	*jardeem bootaneecoo*
both	ambos	*amboosh*
bottlewarmer	aquecedor de biberões	*akessedor duh beeberoynsh*
bottle	garrafa	*garraffa*
box	caixa	*kysha*
box (theatre)	camarote	*cammarot*
boy	rapaz	*rapaj*
bra	soutien	*sootyan*
bracelet	pulseira	*poolsayra*
braised	estufado	*eshtoofardoo*
brake	travão	*travow*
brake fluid	líquido de travões	*leekeedoo duh travoynsh*
brake oil	óleo dos travões	*ollyoo doosh travoynsh*
brass	latão	*latow*
bread	pão	*pow*
break	partir	*parteer*
break-down	avaria do motor	*avaria doo motor*
breakdown service	pronto socorro	*prontoo socorroo*
breakfast	pequeno almoço	*peekaynoo almossoo*
breast	peito	*paytoo*
bridge	ponte	*pont*
bring	trazer	*trazair*
brochure	brochura	*brooshura*
broken	estragado	*eshtragardoo*
broken	partido	*parteedoo*
broth	caldo	*caldoo*
brother	irmão	*irmow*
brown	castanho	*cashtanyoo*
bruise	magoar	*magooar*
brush	escova	*eshcova*
bucket	balde	*balde*
bug	bicho	*beeshoo*
bugs	insectos	*eensetoosh*
building	edifício	*eedifeesyoo*

buoy	bóia	*boya*
bureau de change	casa de câmbio	*caza duh cambyoo*
burglary	assalto	*assaltoo*
burn	queimar	*kaymar*
burn	queimadura	*kaymadoora*
burnt	queimado	*kaymardoo*
bus station	estação de camionetas	*eshtasow duh camyoonetash*
bus stop	paragem de autocarro	*pararjaim duh owtoocahroo*
bus, coach	autocarro	*owtoocahroo*
business class	classe de negócios	*class duh negossyoosh*
business trip	viagem de negócios	*veearjaim duh negossioosh*
busy	atarefado/ocupado	*atarrefardoo/okoopardoo*
butcher	talho	*talyoo*
butter	manteiga	*mantayga*
buttered roll	pãozinho (com manteiga)	*powzeenyoo (com mantayga)*
button	botão	*bootow*
buy	comprar	*comprar*
by airmail	por correio aéreo	*por coorayoo airayoo*

C

cabbage	couve	*cove*
cabin on ship	camarote	*camarot*
café	café	*cafay*
cake	bolinho	*boleenyoo*
cake	bolo	*boloo*
cake shop	pastelaria	*pastellereeah*
call	telefonar	*telefoonar*
called, to be	chamar-se	*shammar-suh*
camera	máquina fotográfica	*markeena fotografeeca*
camp	acampar	*acampar*
camp shop	loja	*lohja*
camp site	campismo	*campeejmoo*
camp site	parque de campismo	*park duh campeejmoo*
camp-fire	fogueira	*foogayra*
camper	carrinha de campismo	*careenya duh campeejmoo*
camping guide	guia de campismo	*gueeah duh campeejmoo*
camping permit	autorização de campismo	*owtoreezasow duh campeejmoo*
canal boat	barco de excursão	*barcoo di eshcoorsow*
cancel	anular	*anoolar*
candle	vela	*vella*
canoe	canoa	*canoah*
canoe	fazer canoagem	*fazzair canooarjaim*
car	automóvel	*owtoomohvel*
car	carruagem	*carruarjaim*
car deck	porão de veículos	*poorow duh vayeecooloosh*
car documents	documentos do carro	*docoomentoosh doo cahroo*
caravan	roulotte	*roolott*
cardigan	casaco	*cazarcoo*
carrot	cenoura	*senora*

cartridge	carga de película fotogrêfica	*carga duh peleecoola fottoograrfeeca*
cash desk	caixa	*kysha*
casino	casino	*cazzeenoo*
cassette	cassette	*cassett*
castle	castelo	*cashteloo*
cat	gato	*gartoo*
catalogue	catálogo	*catalogoo*
cathedral	catedral	*cataydral*
cauliflower	couveflor	*cove flor*
cave	gruta	*groota*
CD	disco compacto (CD)	*deeshcoo compactoo (sayday)*
celebrate	festejar	*feshtayjar*
cemetery	cemitério	*semmeeterryoo*
centimetre	centímetro	*senteemetroo*
central heating	aquecimento central	*akessimentoo centrarl*
centre	(no) meio	*(noo) mayoo*
centre	centro	*centroo*
chair	cadeira	*cadayra*
chambermaid	camareira	*camarayra*
champagne	champanhe	*shampanya*
change	alterar	*alterrar*
change	mudar	*moodar*
change (transit)	fazer transbordo	*fazzair transhbordoo*
change	trocar	*troocar*
change currency	trocar dinheiro	*troocar deenyayroo*
change the baby's nappy	mudar a fralda	*moodar ah fralda*
change the oil	mudar o óleo	*moodar oo ollyoo*
chapel	capela	*capella*
charter flight	vôo charter	*voe shartair*
chat up	paquerar	*pakerrar*
check	ver, controlar	*vair, comtroolar*
check in	fazer o checkin	*fazzair oo sheckeen*
cheers	à saúde	*ah sow-ood*
cheese (tasty, mild)	queijo (bem curado, mal curado)	*kayjoo (baim coorardoo, mal coorardoo)*
chef	cozinheiro-chefe	*coozeenyayroo chef*
chemist	farmácia	*farmassia*
cheque	cheque	*sheck*
cheque card	cartão de cheques	*cartow duh sheksh*
cherries	cerejas	*serayjash*
chess, play	jogar xadrez	*joogar jadrayj*
chewing gum	pastilha elástica/ chiclete	*pashteelya eelashteeca/ cheeclet*
chicken	galinha, frango	*galeenya, frangoo*
child	criança	*creeansa*
child's seat	cadeira para bicicleta	*cadayra parra beeseecletta*
chilled	fresco	*freshcoo*
chin	queixo	*kayshoo*
chips	batatas fritas	*batartash freetash*
chocolate	chocolate	*shoocoolat*
choose	escolher	*eschoolyair*
chop	costeleta	*coshteletta*
christian name	nome	*nom*
church	igreja	*eegrayja*

church service	missa	*meessa*
cigar	charuto	*charootoo*
cigar shop	tabacaria	*tabacareeah*
cigarette	cigarro	*seegarroo*
circle	círculo	*seercooloo*
circus	circo	*seercoo*
city	cidade	*seedard*
city map	planta da cidade	*planta da seedard*
classical concert	concerto de música clássica	*consairtoo duh mooseeca classeeca*
clean	limpo	*leempoo*
clean, to	limpar	*leempar*
clearance	saldo	*saldoo*
closed	fechado	*feshardoo*
clothes	roupa	*roepa*
clothes hanger	cabide	*cabeed*
clothes pegs	molas para a roupa	*mollash parra ah roepa*
clothing	vestuário	*veshtooaryoo*
coat	casaco	*cazarcoo*
cockroach	barata	*barata*
cocoa	cacau	*cackow*
cod	bacalhau fresco	*bacalyow freshcoo*
coffee	café	*cafay*
coffee filter	filtro de café	*feeltroo duh cafay*
cognac	conhaque	*coonyack*
cold (to be)	frio	*freeoo*
cold (to have a)	constipação	*conshteepasow*
collarbone	clavícula	*claveecoola*
colleague	colega	*coolegga*
collision	acidente	*asseedent*
collision	colisão	*cooleezow*
cologne	água de colônia	*agwa duh collonia*
colour	cor	*cor*
colour pencils	lápis de cor	*larpeej duh coor*
colour TV	televisão a cores	*televeesow ah cooresh*
colouring book	livro para colorir	*leevroo parra coloreer*
comb	pente	*pent*
come	vir	*veer*
come back	regressar, voltar	*regressar, voltar*
compartment	compartimento	*compartimentoo*
complaint	dor	*door*
complaint	queixa	*kaysha*
complaints book	livro de reclamações	*leevroo duh reclammasoynsh*
completely	completamente	*completament*
compliment	cumprimento	*coomprimentoo*
compulsory	obrigatório	*obrigatoryoo*
concert	concerto	*consairtoo*
concert hall, theatre	teatro	*teeartroo*
concussion	concussão cerebral	*concoosow cerebral*
condensed milk	leite condensado	*layt condensardoo*
condom	preservativo	*presairvateevoo*
congratulate	felicitar	*feleeceetar*
connection	ligação	*leegasow*
constipation	prisão de ventre	*preezow duh ventre*
consulate	consulado	*consoolardoo*
consultation	consulta	*consoolta*

contact lens	lente de contacto	*lent duh contactoo*
contact lens solution	fluido para lentes de contacto	*flooidoo parra lentsh duh contactoo*
contagious	contagioso	*contajeeozoo*
contraceptive pill	pílula anticoncepcional	*peeloola anttconcepseeoonarl*
cook	cozinheiro	*coozeenyayroo*
cook, to	cozinhar	*coozeenyar*
copper	cobre	*cobbre*
copy	cópia	*cohpia*
corkscrew	sacarolhas	*sacca rollyash*
corn flour	maizena	*myzenna*
corner	canto	*cantoo*
corner	esquina	*eshkeena*
correct	certo	*sairtoo*
correspond	corresponder	*cooreshpondair*
corridor	corredor	*cooredoor*
cot	cama de bebé	*camma duh baybay*
cotton	algodão	*algoodow*
cotton wool	algodão	*algoodow*
cough	tosse	*toss*
cough mixture	xarope para a tosse	*sharopp parra a toss*
country	país	*pyeej*
country	campoo	*campoo*
country code	indicativo do país	*eendeecateevoo*
courgette	courgete	*corjet*
cousin	primo/prima	*preemoo/preema*
crab	caranguejo	*carangayjoo*
cream	creme/natas	*crem/nartash*
credit card	cartão de crédito	*cartow duh credeetoo*
crisps	batatas fritas	*batartash freetash*
croissant	croissant	*croisson*
cross (the road)	atravessar	*atravessar*
crossing	travessia	*travessia*
crossing	passagem	*passarjaim*
cry	chorar	*shoorar*
cubic metre	metro cúbico	*metroo coobeecoo*
cucumber	pepino	*pepeenoo*
cuddly toy	boneco de peluche	*booneckoo duh peloosh*
cuff links	botões de punho	*bootoynsh duh poonyoo*
culottes	saia calça	*syah calsa*
cup	chávena	*sharvena*
curly	encaracolado	*aincarracoolardoo*
current	corrente	*coorent*
cushion	almofadinha	*almoffardeenya*
custard	creme	*crem*
customary	ê costume	*eh coshtoom*
customs	alfândega	*alfandegga*
customs	controle de alfândega	*controll di alfandegga*
cut	cortar	*cortar*
cutlery	talher	*talyair*
cycling	ciclismo	*seecleejmoo*

D

dairy	leiteria	*laytereeah*
damaged	danificado	*danifeecardoo*
dance	dançar	*dansar*
dandruff	caspa	*cashpa*
danger	perigo	*perreegoo*
dangerous	perigoso	*perrigozoo*
dark	escuro	*eshcooroo*
date	encontro	*aincontroo*
daughter	filha	*feelya*
day	dia	*deeah*
day before yesterday	anteontem	*antiontaim*
dead	morto	*mortoo*
decaffeinated	descafeinado	*deshcafaynardoo*
December	dezembro	*dezembroo*
deck chair	cadeira de praia	*cadayra duh prya*
declare (customs)	declarar	*declarar*
deep	profundo	*proofoondoo*
deep sea diving	mergulho	*mairgoolyoo*
deepfreeze	congelador	*conjellador*
degrees	graus	*graush*
delay	atraso	*atrarzoo*
delicatessen	charcutaria	*sharcootareeah*
delicious	saboroso	*saborohzoo*
delicious	delicioso	*delisseeohzoo*
dentist	dentista	*denteeshta*
dentures	dentadura	*dentadoora*
deodorant	desodorizante	*desodoreezant*
department	secção	*secksow*
department store	armazém	*armazaim*
departure	partida	*parteeda*
departure time	hora de partida	*ora duh parteeda*
depilatory cream	creme depilatório	*crem depeelatoryoo*
deposit	sinal	*seenal*
dessert	sobremesa	*sobremayza*
destination	destino	*deshteenoo*
destiny	destino	*deshteenoo*
develop	revelar	*revelar*
diabetic	diabético	*deeabeteecoo*
dial	marcar	*marcar*
dialling code	indicativo	*eendeecateevoo*
diamond	diamante	*deeamant*
diarrhoea	diarreia	*deearraya*
dictionary	dicionário	*deesionaryoo*
diesel	diesel	*deezel*
diesel oil	gasóleo	*gazollyoo*
diet	dieta	*deeayta*
difficulty	dificuldade	*deefeeculdard*
dining room	sala de jantar	*sarla duh jantar*
dining/buffet car	vagão restaurante	*vagow reshtowrant*
dinner	jantar	*jantar*
dinner jacket	smoking	*smockeeng*
direction	direcção	*deeressow*
directly	directo	*deerectoo*
dirty	sujo	*soojoo*
disabled	inválido	*eenvalleedoo*
disco	discoteca	*deeshcooteca*

discount	desconto	*deshcontoo*
dish	prato	*prartoo*
dish of the day	prato do dia	*prartoo doo deeah*
disinfectant	desinfectante	*dezeenfectant*
distance	distância	*deeshtarncia*
distilled water	água destilada	*agwa deshteelarda*
disturb	incomodar	*eencoomoodar*
disturbance	perturbação	*pairtoorbasow*
diving	mergulhar	*mairgoolyar*
diving board	prancha de saltos	*pransha duh saltoosh*
diving gear	equipamento para mergulhar	*ekeepamentoo parra mairgoolyar*
divorced	divorciado	*deevorceeardoo*
DIY shop	loja faça-você-mesmo	*loja fassa vossay mejmoo*
dizzy	tonto	*tontoo*
do	fazer	*fazzair*
doctor	médico	*mehdeecoo*
dog	cão	*cow*
doll	boneca	*booneca*
domestic	doméstico	*doomehsteecoo*
door	porta	*porta*
double bed	cama de casal	*camma duh cazal*
down	em baixo	*aim byshoo*
draught	corrente de ar	*coorent di ar*
dream	sonhar	*soonyar*
dress	vestido	*veshteedoo*
dressing gown	roupão	*roepow*
drink	bebida	*bebbeeda*
drink	beber	*bebbair*
drinking chocolate	leite com chocolate	*layt com shoocoolat*
drinking water	água potável	*agwa pootarvel*
drive	conduzir	*condoozeer*
drive	motorista	*motoreeshta*
driving licence	carta de condução	*carta duh condoosow*
drought	seca	*sayca*
dry	secar	*seccar*
dry	seco	*saycoo*
dry clean	limpar a seco	*leempar ah saycoo*
dry cleaner's	limpeza a seco	*leempayza ah saycoo*
dry shampoo	champô seco	*shampoh saycoo*
dummy	chupeta	*shoopeta*
during	durante	*doorant*
during the day	durante o dia	*doorant oo deeah*
duty free shop	loja franca	*loja franca*

E

ear	orelha/ouvido	*orelya/ohveedoo*
ear, nose and throat specialist	otorrinolaringo-logista	*otorreenoolareengoloo-jeeshta*
earache	dor de ouvidos	*door duh oeveedoosh*
eardrops	gotas para os ouvidos	*gotash parra ooz oeveedoosh*
early	cedo	*saydoo*
earrings	brincos	*breencoosh*
earth	terra	*tehrah*
earthenware	cerâmica	*serrameeca*

east	este	*esht*
easy	fácil	*farseel*
eat	comer	*comair*
eczema	eczema	*eczma*
eel	enguia	*aingueeah*
egg	ovo	*ohvoo*
elastic band	elástico	*elashteecoo*
electric	eléctrico	*eletreecoo*
electricity	electricidade	*eletreesidard*
embassy	embaixada	*embysharda*
emergency brake	alarme	*alarm*
emergency exit	saída de emergência	*syeeda duh emairjensia*
emergency number	número de alarme	*noomeroo duh alarm*
emergency phone	telefone de emergência	*telefon duh emairjensia*
emergency triangle	triângulo de emergência	*treeangooloo duh emairjensia*
emery board	lima de unhas	*leema duh oonyash*
empty	vazio	*vazeeoo*
engaged	ocupado	*ocupardoo*
England	Inglaterra	*eenglaterra*
English, Englishman	inglês	*eenglayj*
enjoy	ter prazer	*tair prezzair*
entertainment (show) event	espectáculo	*espetarcooloo*
entertainment guide	revista de espectáculos	*reveeshta duh espetarcooloosh*
envelope	envelope	*envellop*
escort	acompanhante	*acompanyant*
evening (before 6pm)	tarde	*tard*
evening wear	traje de noite	*trarge duh noyt*
everything	tudo	*toodoo*
everywhere	por toda a parte	*por toeda ah part*
examine	examinar	*eezameenar*
excavations	escavações	*eshcavasoynsh*
excellent	óptimo	*otteemoo*
exchange	trocar	*troocar*
exchange rate	câmbio	*cambyoo*
excursion	excursão	*eshcoorsow*
exhibition	exposição	*eshpozisow*
exit	saida	*syeeda*
expenses	despesas	*deshpayzash*
expensive	caro	*caroo*
explain	explicar	*eeshpleecar*
express	comboio rápido	*comboyoo rapeedoo*
external	externo	*eeshtairnoo*
eye	olho	*olyoo*
eyedrops	gotas para os olhos	*gotash parra ooz olyoosh*
eyeshadow	sombra	*sombra*
eye specialist	oftalmologista	*oftalmolojeeshta*
eyeliner	lápis para os olhos	*larpeesh parra ooz olyoosh*

F

face	cara	*cara*
factory	fábrica	*fabreeca*
fair	feira	*fayra*

fall	cair	*kyeer*
family	famÌlia	*fameelia*
famous	famoso	*famozoo*
far away	longe	*lonj*
farm	quinta	*keenta*
farmer	agricultor	*agreecooltor*
farmer's wife	mulher do agricultor	*moolyair do agreecooltor*
fashion	moda	*mohda*
fast	rápido	*rapeedoo*
father	pai	*pie*
fault	culpa	*coolpa*
fax, send a	enviar um fax	*enveear oom fax*
February	fevereiro	*fevverayroo*
feel	sentir	*senteer*
feel like	ter vontade	*tair vontard*
fence	vedação	*veddasow*
ferry	barco	*barcoo*
fever	febre	*febre*
fill a tooth	obturar um dente	*obtoorar oom dent*
fill out	preencher	*pree-enshair*
filling	obturaçâo	*obtoorasow*
film	rolo fotográfico	*rolloo fotoograrfeecoo*
film	filme	*feelm*
filter	filtro	*feeltroo*
find	achar	*ashar*
fine	multa	*moolta*
finger	dedo	*daydoo*
fire	fogueira	*foogayra*
fire	incêndio	*eensendyoo*
fire brigade	bombeiros	*bombayroosh*
fire escape	escada de emergência	*eshcarda duh emmairjensia*
fire extinguisher	extintor	*eshteentor*
first	primeiro	*preemayroo*
first aid	primeiros socorros	*preemayroosh socorroosh*
first class	primeira classe	*preemayra class*
fish, to	pescar	*peshcar*
fish	peixe	*paysh*
fishing rod	cana de pesca	*carna duh peshca*
fit	assentar	*assentar*
fitness centre	centro de manutenção física	*sentroo duh manootensow feeseeca*
fitness training	treino de manutenção física	*traynoo duh manootensow feeseeca*
fitting room	gabinete de prova	*gabeenet duh provva*
fix/stick	colar/consertar	*coollar/consairtar*
flag	bandeira	*bandayra*
flash bulb	lâmpada do flash	*lamparda doo flash*
flash cube	flash em cubo	*flash aim cooboo*
flea market	feira da ladra	*fayra da ladra*
flight	vôo	*voe*
flight number	número do vôo	*noomeroo duh voe*
flood	inundaçâo	*eenoondasow*
floor (building)	andar	*andar*
flour	farinha	*fareenya*
flyover	viaduto	*veeadootoo*
fly (insect)	mosca	*moshca*

fly (verb)	voar	*vooar*
fog	nevoeiro	*nevooayroo*
folding caravan	atrelado	*atrelardoo*
folkloric	folclórico	*folclorreecoo*
follow	seguir	*segear*
food	alimento	*allymentoo*
food poisoning	intoxicação alimentar	*eentoxeecasow allimentar*
foot	pé	*peh*
for	para	*parra*
for hire	aluga-se	*alooga-suh*
forbidden	proibido	*prooeebeedoo*
forehead	testa	*teshta*
foreign	estrangeiro	*eshtranjayroo*
forget	esquecer	*eshkessair*
fork	garfo	*garfoo*
form	impresso	*eempressoo*
fort	fortaleza	*fortalayza*
forward, send	enviar	*ainveeyar*
fountain	fonte	*font*
frame	armação	*armasow*
frank	franco	*francoo*
free	livre	*leevre*
free	gratuito	*gratooeetoo*
free time	tempo livre	*tempoo leevre*
freeze	congelar	*conjelar*
French	francês	*fransayj*
fresh	fresco	*freshcoo*
Friday	sexta-feira	*seshta fayra*
fried	frito	*freetoo*
fried egg	ovo estrelado	*ovoo shtrelardoo*
friend	amigo	*ameegoo*
friendly	simpático	*seemparteecoo*
friendly	amigavel	*ameegarvel*
fright	medo	*maydoo*
fringe	franja	*franja*
fruit	fruta	*froota*
fruit juice	sumo de frutas	*soomoo duh frootash*
frying pan	frigideira	*freejeedayra*
full	cheio	*shayoo*
fun	divertimento	*deevairteementoo*

G

gallery	galeria	*gallereea*
game	jogo	*jogoo*
garage	garagem	*gararjaim*
garden	jardim	*jardeem*
gastroenteritis	gastrenterite	*gashtrentaireet*
gauze	gaze	*gaz*
gear	velocidade	*velossidard*
gel	gel	*jel*
German	alemão	*allaymow*
get married	casar-se	*cazar-suh*
get off (e.g. a bus)	sair	*syeer*
gift	presente	*present*
gilt	dourado	*doorardoo*
ginger	gengibre	*jenjeebre*
girl	rapariga	*rapareega*

girlfriend	amiga	*ameega*
giro cheque	cheque dos correios	*sheck doosh coorayoosh*
giro guarantee card	cartão dos correios	*cartow doosj coorayoosh*
glass (for drinking)	copo	*copoo*
glass (window)	vidro	*veedroo*
glasses (sun-)	óculos (de sol)	*ocooloosh (duh sol)*
glide	planar	*plannar*
glove	luva	*loova*
glue	cola	*colla*
gnat	mosquito	*moshkeetoo*
go	ir	*ear*
go back	regressar	*regressar*
go out	sair	*syeer*
goat's cheese	queijo de cabra	*cayjoo duh cabra*
gold	ouro	*oroo*
golf course	campo de golfe	*campoo duh golf*
gone	perdido	*pairdeedoo*
good afternoon	boa tarde	*boa tard*
good evening	boa noite	*boa noyt*
good morning	bom dia	*bom deeah*
good night	boa noite	*boa noyt*
goodbye	adeus	*adayoosh*
goodbye	despedida	*deshpedeeda*
gram	grama	*grarma*
grams	gramas	*grarmash*
grandchild	neto/neta	*netoo/neta*
grandfather	avô	*avoe*
grandmother	avó	*avoh*
grape juice	sumo de uva	*soomoo di oova*
grapefruit	toranja	*tooranja*
grapes	uvas	*oovash*
grave	sepultura	*sepooltoora*
grease	gordura	*gordoora*
green	verde	*vaird*
green card	cartão verde	*cartow vaird*
greet	cumprimentar	*coompreementar*
grey haired	grisalho	*grizalyoo*
grill	grelhar	*grelyar*
grilled	grelhado	*grelyardoo*
grocer's shop	mercearia	*mercyareeah*
groceries	artigos de mercearia	*arteegoosh duh maircyareeah*
ground	chão	*shau*
ground beef	carne picada	*carn peecarda*
group	grupo	*groopoo*
guest house	pensão	*pensow*
guide (person, book)	guía	*gueeah*
guided tour	viagem guiada	*veearjaim gueearda*
gynaecologist	ginecologista	*jeenaycolojeeshta*

H

hair	cabelo	*cabayloo*
hairbrush	escova de cabelo	*eshcova duh cabayloo*
hairdresser	cabeleireiro, barbeiro	*cabelayrayroo, barbayroo*
hairpins	ganchos de cabelo	*ganshoosh duh cabayloo*
hairspray	laca para o cabelo	*laca parra oo cabayloo*
hairstyle	penteado	*pentyardoo*

half	meio	*mayoo*
half	metade	*metard*
half full	meio cheio	*mayoo shayoo*
hammer	martelo	*martelloo*
hand	mão	*mau*
handbrake	travão de mão	*travow duh mau*
handbag	mala	*mala*
handicrafts	artesanato	*artesanartoo*
handkerchief	lenço	*lensoo*
handmade	feito à mão	*faytoo ah mau*
happy	alegre	*allegre*
harbour	porto	*portoo*
hard	duro	*dooroo*
hat	chapéu	*shapayoo*
have dinner	jantar	*jantar*
hayfever	febre do feno	*febre doo fennoo*
hazelnut	avelã	*avelar*
head	cabeça	*cabaysa*
headache	dor de cabeça	*door duh cabaysa*
health	saúde	*sow-ood*
health food shop	loja de artigos dietéticos	*loja duh arteegoosh dee-eteteecoosh*
hear	perceber	*pairsebbair*
hearing aid	aparelho auditivo	*aparellyoo owdeeteevoo*
heart	coração	*coorasow*
heart patient	cardlaco	*cardeeacoo*
heater	aquecimento	*akessimentoo*
heavy	pesado	*pezardoo*
heel	calcanhar	*calcanyar*
heel (shoe)	salto	*saltoo*
hello	óla	*ohla*
hello	viva	*veeva*
helmet	capacete	*cappaset*
help	ajudar	*ajoodar*
help	ajuda	*ajooda*
helping	dose	*doz*
herbal tea	chá de ervas	*shar di airvash*
herbs	ervas	*airvash*
here	aqui	*akee*
here you have	aqui tem	*akee taim*
herring	arenque	*arenk*
high	alto	*altoo*
high tide	maré cheia	*maray shaya*
highchair	cadeira de bebé	*cadayra duh baybay*
hiking	andar a pé	*andar ah peh*
hiking trip	excursão	*eshcoorsow ah peh*
hip	anca	*anca*
hire	alugar	*aloogar*
hitchhike	pedir boleia	*pedeer bolaya*
hobby	hobby	*obby*
holdup	assalto	*assaltoo*
holiday	feriado	*ferriardoo*
holiday	férias	*ferryash*
holiday house	casa de férias	*carza duh ferriash*
holiday village	aldeamento turístico	*aldayamentoo tooreeshteecoo*
homesickness	saudades	*sowdardesh*

honest	honesto	*hooneshtoo*
honey	mel	*mel*
horizontal	horizontal	*oreezontarl*
horrible	horroroso	*ororohzoo*
horse	cavalo	*cavarloo*
hospital	hospital	*oshpeetarl*
hospitality	hospitalidade	*oshpeetalidad*
hot	quente	*kent*
hotwater bottle	botija	*booteeja*
hot	picante	*peecant*
hotel	hotel	*ottel*
hour	hora	*oara*
house	casa	*carza*
household items	artigos domésticos	*arteegoosh doomeshteecoosh*
houses of parliament	edifício parlamentar	*edeefeesyoo parlamentar*
housewife	dona de casa	*donna duh carza*
how far?	a que distância?	*ah kay deeshtancia*
how long?	quanto tempo?	*cuarntoo tempoo?*
how much?	quanto?	*cuarntoo?*
how?	como?	*cohmoo?*
hurricane	ciclone	*seeeclon*
hurry	pressa	*pressa*
husband	marido	*mareedoo*
hut	cabana	*cabarna*
hyperventilation	hiperventilação	*eepairventeelasow*

I

ice cubes	cubos de gelo	*cooboosh duh jayloo*
icecream	gelado	*jelardoo*
idea	ideia	*eedaya*
identification	documento de identificação	*docoomentoo duh identeefeecasow*
identify	identificar	*eedenteefeecar*
ignition key	chave de contacto	*sharv duh contactoo*
ill	doente	*dooent*
illness	doença	*dooensa*
imagine	imaginar	*eemajeenar*
immediately	imediatamente	*eemediatament*
import duty	direito de importação	*deeraytoo di eemportasow*
impossible	impossível	*eempoosseevel*
impressions	impressões	*eempressoynsh*
in	dentro	*dentroo*
in the evening	à noitinha	*ah noyteenya*
in the morning	de manhã	*duh manyar*
included	incluído	*eenclooydoo*
included	inclusivo	*eenclooseevoo*
indicate	apontar	*appontar*
indicator	placa de sinalização	*placa duh seenaleezasow*
inexpensive	barato	*barartoo*
infection (viral/ bacterial)	infecção (virótica/ bacteriana)	*eenfecksow (veeroteeca/ bacteriana)*
inflammation	inflamação	*eenflammasow*
influenza	gripe	*greep*
information	informação	*eenformasow*

information	dados	*dardoosh*
information desk	balcão de informações	*balcow di eenformasoynsh*
injection	injecção	*eenjecksow*
injured	ferido	*ferreedoo*
inner tube	câmara de ar	*cammara di ar*
innocent	inocente	*eenoocent*
insect	insecto	*eensectoo*
insect bite	picadela de insecto	*peecadella di eensectoo*
insect repellant	repellente contra mosquitos	*repellent contra moshkeetoosh*
inside	dentro	*dentroo*
insole	palmilha	*palmeelya*
instructions	instruções	*eenshtroosoynsh*
insurance	seguro	*segooroo*
intermission	intervalo	*eentervarloo*
international	internacional	*eentairnacionarl*
interpreter	intérprete	*eentairpret*
intersection	cruzamento	*croozamentoo*
introduce oneself	apresentar-se	*aprezentar-suh*
invite	convidar	*conveedar*
iodine	iodo	*yod*
Ireland	Irlanda	*earlanda*
iron	ferro	*fehroo*
iron, to	passar a ferro	*passar ah ferroo*
iron	ferro de passar	*ferroo duh passar*
ironing board	tábua de passar	*tabooah duh passar*
island	ilha	*eelya*
Italian	italiano	*eetaliarnoo*
itch	comichão	*comeechow*

J

jack, monkey	macaco	*makarkoo*
jacket	casaco curto	*cazarcoo coortoo*
jam	doce	*dose*
January	janeiro	*janayroo*
jaw	maxilar	*maksilar*
jellyfish	alforreca	*alfoorecka*
jeweller	joalharia	*jooalyareeah*
jewellery	jóias	*joyash*
jog	fazer jogging	*fazzair joggeeng*
joke	piada	*peearda*
juice	sumo	*soomoo*
July	julho	*joolyoo*
jump leads	cabos para ligar a bateria	*carboosh parra leegar a batereeah*
jumper	camisola	*cameezola*
June	junho	*joonyoo*

K

key	chave	*sharv*
kilo	quilo	*keeloo*
kilometre	quilómetro	*keelometroo*
king	rei	*ray*
kiosk	quiosque	*keeoshk*
kiss (verb)	beijar	*bayjar*
kiss	beijo	*bayjoo*

kitchen	cozinha	*coozeenya*
knee	joelho	*jooelyoo*
knee socks	meias até o joelho	*mayash atay ow jooelyoo*
knife	faca	*facca*
knit	tricotar	*treecootar*
know	saber	*sabair*

L

lace	renda	*renda*
lace (shoe)	atacador	*attackadoor*
ladies'	lavabos de senhoras	*lavarboosh duh senyorash*
lake	lago	*largoo*
lamp	lâmpada	*lamparda*
land	terra	*terra*
lane	faixa de rodagem	*fysha duh roodarjaim*
language	língua	*leengwa*
large	grande	*grand*
last (previous)	anterior	*anterrior*
last	último	*oolteemoo*
last night	ontem à noite	*ontaim ah noyt*
late	tarde	*tard*
later, already	já	*jah*
laugh	rir	*rear*
launderette	lavandaria	*lavandareeah*
law	direito	*diraytoo*
laxative	purgativo	*poorgateevoo*
leak	furo	*fooroo*
leather	pele/couro	*pel/cooroo*
leather goods	artigos de pele	*arteegoosh duh pel*
leave	partir	*parteer*
leek	alho francês	*alyoo fransayj*
left	esquerda	*eshcairda*
left	à esquerda	*ah eshcairda*
left luggage	depósito de bagagem	*depozzeetoo duh bagarjaim*
leg	perna	*pairna*
lemon	limão	*leemow*
lend	emprestar	*aimpreshtar*
lens	lente	*lent*
lentils	lentilhas	*lenteelyash*
less	menos	*menoosh*
lesson	lição	*leesow*
letter	carta	*carta*
lettuce	alface	*alfass*
level crossing	passagem de nível	*passarjaim duh neevel*
library	biblioteca	*beebleeootehca*
lie	mentir	*menteer*
lie	deitarse	*daytarse*
lift (hitchhike)	boleia	*boolaya*
lift (in building)	elevador	*eelevadoor*
light (not dark)	claro	*claroo*
light (not heavy)	leve	*lev*
light	luz	*loosh*
light, to	acender	*assendair*
lighter	isqueiro	*eeshkayroo*
lighthouse	farol	*farol*
lightning	raio	*ryoo*

like	gostar de	*goshtar duh*
line	linha	*leenya*
linen	linho	*leenyoo*
lipstick	batôn	*baton*
liqueur	licor	*leecor*
liquorice	alcaçuz	*alcasooj*
listen	ouvir	*ohveer*
literature	literatura	*leeteratoora*
litre	litro	*leetroo*
little	pouco	*pohcoo*
live	morar	*moorar*
live together	viver junto	*veevair joontoo*
lobster	lagosta	*lagoshta*
local	local	*loocal*
lock	fechadura	*feshadoora*
long	comprido	*compreedoo*
long lasting	de longa duração	*duh longa doorasow*
look	olhar	*oolyar*
look for	procurar	*procoorar*
lorry	camião	*cammyow*
lose	perder	*pairdair*
loss	perda	*pairda*
lost	perdido	*pairdeedoo*
lost property office	achados e perdidos	*ashardoosh ee perdeedooz*
lotion	loção	*loosow*
loud	alto	*altoo*
love, to	gostar/amar	*goshtar/amar*
love	amor	*amor*
low	baixo	*byshoo*
low tide	maré baixa	*maray bysha*
luck	sorte	*sort*
luggage	bagagem	*bagarjaim*
luggage locker	cofre de bagagem	*cofre duh bagarjaim*
lunch	almoço	*almoesoo*
lungs	pulmões	*poolmoynsh*

M

macaroni	macarrão	*macarrow*
machine (vending)	vendedor automático	*vendador owtoomateecoo*
madam	senhora	*senyora*
magazine	revista	*reveeshta*
mail	correio	*coorayoo*
main post office	correio central	*coorayoo centrarl*
main road	estrada	*eshtrarda*
make an appointment	marcar um encontro	*marcar oom aincontroo*
make love	fazer amor	*fazzair amor*
makeshift	provisório	*prooveesoryoo*
man	homem	*omaim*
manager	gerente	*jerrent*
mandarin	tangerina	*tanjereena*
manicure	manicure	*manicure*
map	mapa	*mapa*
marble	mármore	*marmora*
March	março	*marsoo*

margarine	margarina	*margareena*
marina	marina	*mareena*
market	mercado	*mercardoo*
marriage, wedding	casamento	*cazamento*
married	casado	*cazardoo*
mass	missa	*meessa*
massage	massagem	*massarjaim*
matt	sem brilho	*saim breelyoo*
match	desafio/jogo	*dezafyoo/jogoo*
matches	fósforos	*foshforoosh*
May	maio	*myoo*
maybe	talvez	*talvayj*
mayonnaise	maionese	*myonez*
mayor	presidente da câmara/prefeito	*prezeedent da cammara/preffaytoo*
meal	refeição	*refaysow*
mean	significar	*seegneefeecar*
meat	carne	*carn*
medication, medicine	medicamento/ remédio	*medicamentoo/ remedyoo*
meet	conhecer	*coonyessair*
melon	melão	*melow*
membership	adesão	*adezow*
menstruate	menstruar	*menshtrooar*
menstruation	menstruação	*menshtruasow*
menu	menu, ementa	*menoo, ementa*
menu of the day	menu do dia	*menoo doo dia*
message	mensagem	*mensarjaim*
metal	metal	*mettal*
meter	taxímetro	*tackseemetroo*
metre	metro	*metroo*
migraine	enxaqueca	*ainshakeka*
milk	leite	*layt*
millimetre	milímetro	*meeleemetroo*
milometer	contaquilómetros	*conta keelometroosh*
mineral water	água mineral	*agwa meeneral*
minute	minuto	*meenootoo*
mirror	espelho	*shpelyoo*
miss	sentir a falta	*senteer ah falta*
missing person	desaparecido	*dezaparesseedoo*
mistake	erro	*ehroo*
mistake	engano	*aingarnoo*
misunderstanding	malentendido	*mal entendeedoo*
mixture	mistura	*meeshtoora*
modern art	arte moderna	*art mooderna*
molar	molar	*moolar*
moment	um momento	*oom momentoo*
monastery	mosteiro	*mooshtayroo*
Monday	segunda-feira	*segoonda fayra*
money	dinheiro	*deenyayroo*
month	mês	*mayj*
moped	bicicleta motorizada	*beeceecletta mottooreezarda*
more and more	cada vez mais	*cadda vaij mysh*
morning-after pill	pílula 'morning after'	*peeloola 'morning-after'*
mosque	mesquita	*meshkeeta*
motel	motel	*mohtel*

mother	mãe	*my*
motor cross	motociclismo	*motooseecleejmoo*
motorbike	motocicleta	*motooseeclayta*
motorboat	barco a motor	*barcoo ah motor*
motorway	autoestrada	*owtooshtrarda*
mountain	monte	*mont*
mountain hut	refúgio	*refoogyoo*
mountaineering	alpinismo	*alpeeneejmoo*
mountaineering shoes	sapatos de alpinismo	*sapartoosh duh alpeeneejmoo*
mouse	rato	*rartoo*
mouth	boca	*boca*
much/many	muito/muitos	*mweentoo/mweentoosh*
multistorey car park	parque de vários andares	*park duh varyooz andaresh*
muscle	músculo	*mooshcooloo*
muscle spasms	cãibras	*kybraj*
museum	museu	*moosayoo*
mushrooms	cogumelos	*cogoomeloosh*
music	música	*mooseeca*
musical	musical	*mooseecal*
mussels	mexilhões	*mesheelyoynsh*
mustard	mostarda	*mooshtarda*

N

nail	unha	*oonya*
nail (metal)	prego	*praygoo*
nail polish	verniz para as unhas	*verneej parra az oonyash*
nail polish remover	acetona para as unhas	*assaytona parra az oonyash*
nail scissors	tesoura de unhas	*tezora di oonyash*
naked	nu	*noo*
nappy	fralda	*fralda*
nationality	nacionalidade	*nasionaleedad*
natural	naturalmente	*natooralment*
nature	natureza	*natoorayza*
naturism	naturismo	*natooreejmoo*
naturist beach	praia de naturistas	*prya duh natooreeshtash*
nauseous	enjoativo	*ainjooateevoo*
near	perto de	*pairtoo duh*
nearby	perto	*pairtoo*
necessary	necessário	*necessaryoo*
neck	pescoço	*peshcossoo*
necklace	fio	*feeoo*
nectarine	nectarina	*nectareena*
needle	agulha	*agoolya*
negative	negativo	*negateevoo*
neighbours	vizinhos	*veezeenyoosh*
nephew	sobrinho	*soobreenyoo*
never	nunca	*noonca*
new	novo	*nohvoo*
news	notícias	*nooteeciash*
newspaper	jornal	*jornal*
next	seguinte	*segeent*
next to	ao lado	*ow lardoo*
nice (friendly)	simpático	*seemparteecoo*
nice (to taste)	agradável, bonito	*agradarvel, booneetoo*

niece	sobrinha	*soobreenya*
night	noite	*noyt*
night duty	serviço nocturno	*sairveesoo noctoornoo*
nightclub	clube nocturno	*cloob noctoornoo*
nightlife	vida nocturna	*veeda noctoorna*
no one	ninguém	*neengaim*
no	não	*now*
no overtaking	proibido de ultrapassar	*prooeebeedoo duh ooltrapassar*
noise	barulho	*baroolyoo*
nonstop	directo (sem paragens)	*deerectoo (saim pararjainsh)*
normal	normal	*normal*
north	norte	*nort*
nose	nariz	*nareej*
nose drops	gotas para o nariz	*gotash parra oo nareej*
notepaper	papel de escrever	*papel duh eshcrevair*
nothing	nada	*narda*
November	novembro	*noovembroo*
nowhere	em parte nenhuma	*aim part nenyooma*
number	número	*noomeroo*
number plate	matrícula	*matreecoola*
nurse	enfermeira	*ainfairmayra*
nutmeg	noz moscada	*noj mooshcarda*
nuts (mixed)	nozes (mistura)	*nozesh (meeshtoora)*

O

October	outubro	*ohtoobroo*
offer	oferecer	*ofressair*
office	escritório	*eshcreetoryoo*
oil	óleo	*ollyoo*
oil level	nível do óleo	*neevel doo ollyoo*
ointment	pomada	*poomarda*
ointment for burns	pomada contra queimaduras	*poomarda contra kaymadurash*
okay	de acordo	*di acordoo*
old	velho	*velyoo*
olive oil	azeite	*azayt*
olives	azeitonas	*azaytonash*
omelette	omeleta	*omelayta*
on	em cima de	*aim seema duh*
on board	a bordo	*ah bordoo*
on the right	direito	*diraytoo*
on the way	no caminho	*noo cameenyoo*
oncoming car	em sentido contrário	*aim senteedoo contraryoo*
oneway traffic	trânsito de sentido único	*transeetoo duh senteedoo ooneecoo*
onion	cebola	*sebolla*
open	aberto	*abairtoo*
open	abrir	*abreer*
opera	ópera	*opera*
operate	operar	*operar*
operator (telephone)	telefonista	*telefoneeshta*
operetta	opereta	*operetta*
opposite	em frente	*aim frent*
optician	oculista	*occooleeshta*
orange (colour)	cor de laranja	*coor duh laranja*

orange	laranja	*laranja*
orange juice	sumo de laranja	*soomoo duh laranja*
order (in -,) tidy	em ordem	*aim ordaim*
order	encomenda	*aincoomenda*
order, to	encomendar	*aincoomendar*
other	outro	*ohtroo*
other side	do outro lado	*doo ohtroo lardoo*
outside	fora	*forra*
overtake	ultrapassar	*ooltrapassar*
oysters	ostras	*oshtrash*

P

packed lunch	merenda/lanche	*merenda/lansh*
packet (of cigarettes)	pacote (de cigarros)	*packot (duh seegarroosh)*
page	página	*parjeena*
pain	dor	*door*
painkiller	analgésico	*analjezeecoo*
paint	tinta	*teenta*
painting	pintura	*peentoora*
palace	palácio	*palassio*
pan	panela	*panella*
pancake	crepe	*crep*
pane	vidro	*veedroo*
pants, briefs, knickers	cuecas	*cooeckash*
panty liner	penso de protecção	*pensoo duh prootecsow*
paper	papel	*papel*
paprika	pimento	*peementoo*
paraffin oil	petróleo	*petrollyoo*
parasol	chapéu de sol	*shapayoo duh sol*
parcel	encomenda postal	*aimcoomenda pooshtal*
parcel	pacote	*packot*
pardon	desculpe	*deshcoolp*
parents	pais	*pysh*
park	parque	*park*
park	estacionar	*estassionar*
parking space	lugar para estacionar	*loogar parra eshtassionar*
parsley	salsa	*salsa*
part (car)	peça	*pessa*
partition	separação	*separação*
partner	companheiro	*companyayroo*
party	festa	*feshta*
passable (road)	transitável	*transeetarvel*
passenger	passageiro	*passajayroo*
passport	passaporte	*passaport*
passport photo	foto tipo passe	*fotoo teepoo pass*
patient	doente	*dooent*
pavement	passeio/calçada	*passayoo/calsarda*
pay	pagar	*paggar*
pay the bill	pagar a conta	*pagar a conta*
peach	pêssego	*pessaygoo*
peanuts	amendoins	*amendooeensh*
pear	pera	*paira*
peas	ervilhas	*airveelyash*
pedal	pedalo	*pedarloo*
pedestrian crossing	passagem para peões	*passarjaim parra peeoynsh*

pedicure	pedicure	*pedicure*
pen	caneta	*canetta*
pencil (hard/soft)	lápis (duro/macio)	*larpeej (dooroo/maseeyoo)*
penis	pénis	*penneej*
penknife	canivete	*canivet*
pepper	pimenta	*peementa*
performance (show)	representação	*representasow*
perfume	perfume	*perfoom*
perm	permanente	*permanent*
perm, to have a...	fazer uma permanente	*fazzair ooma permanent*
permit	licença	*leesensa*
person	pessoa	*pessoa*
personal	pessoal	*pessoal*
petrol	gasolina	*gazooleena*
petrol station	estação de serviço/ posto de gasolina	*eshtasow duh serveesoo/ poshtoo duh gazooleena*
pets	animais de estimação	*animysh duh eshteemasow*
pharmacy	farmácia	*farmassia*
phone (tele-)	telefone	*telefon*
phone (verb)	telefonar	*telefoonar*
phone box	cabine telefónica	*cabeen telefoneeca*
phone directory	lista telefónica	*leeshta telefoneeca*
phone number	número de telefone	*noomeroo duh telefon*
photo	fotografia	*fotografeea*
photocopier	máquina copiadora	*markeena copiadoora*
photocopy (verb)	fotocopiar	*fotoocoopiar*
photocopy	fotocópia	*fotoocopia*
pick up	ir buscar	*ear booshcar*
picnic	piquenique	*peekneek*
piece of clothing	peça de roupa	*pessa duh roepa*
pier	pontão/cais	*pontow/kysh*
pigeon	pombo	*pomboo*
pill (contraceptive)	pílula anticoncepcional	*peeloola anticonsepcional*
pillow	almofada	*almoofarda*
pillowcase	fronha	*fronya*
pin	alfinete	*alfeenet*
pineapple	ananás	*ananash*
pipe	cachimbo	*casheemboo*
pipe tobacco	tabaco para cachimbo	*tabacoo parra casheemboo*
pity	(ter) pena	*(tair) penna*
place of interest	lugares turísticos	*loogaresh tooreeshteecoosh*
plan	planta	*planta*
plant	planta	*planta*
plasters	pensos	*pensoosh*
plastic	plástico	*plashteecoo*
plate, dish, course	prato	*prartoo*
platform	linha	*leenya*
platform	cais	*kysh*
play, (theatre)	peça de teatro	*pessa duh teeartroo*
play	brincar	*breencar*
play basketball	jogar basquetebol	*joogar bashketboll*

play draughts	jogar às damas	*joogar as damash*
play golf	jogar golfe	*joogar golf*
play tennis	jogar ténis	*joogar teneej*
playground	jardim infantil	*jardeem eenfanteel*
playing cards	cartas de jogar	*cartash duh joogar*
pleasant	agradável	*agradarvel*
please	se faz favor	*suh faj favvor*
pleasure	prazer	*prazzair*
plum	ameixa	*amaysha*
point	indicar	*eendeecar*
poison	veneno	*venenoo*
police	polícia	*poleesia*
police station	posto da polícia	*poshtoo da poleesia*
police officer	polícia	*poleesia*
pond	tanque	*tank*
pony	pónei	*pohnay*
pop concert	concerto de pop	*consairtoo duh pop*
population	população	*poopoolasow*
pork	carne de porco	*carn duh porcoo*
port-wine	vinho do Porto	*veenyoo doo portoo*
porter	bagageiro	*bagajayroo*
porter	porteiro	*portayroo*
post code	código postal	*codeegoo pooshtal*
post office	agência do correio	*ajencia do coorayoo*
postage	porte	*port*
postbox	caixa de correio	*kysha duh coorayoo*
postcard	postal	*pooshtal*
postman	carteiro	*cartayroo*
potato	batata	*batarta*
poultry	aves	*arvesh*
pound	libra	*leebra*
powdered milk	leite em pó	*layt aim poh*
power point	ligação eléctrica/ tomada	*leegasow eeletreeca/ toomarda*
pram	carrinho de bébé	*carreenyoo duh baybay*
prawns	camarões	*cammaroynsh*
precious	precioso	*pressiozoo*
prefer, to	preferir	*prefereer*
preference	preferência	*preferensia*
pregnant	grávida	*graveeda*
present	presente	*prezzent*
pressure	stress	*shtress*
price	preço	*praysoo*
price list	lista de preços	*leeshta duh praysoosh*
print	imprimir	*eempreemeer*
print (verb)	fazer cópias	*fazair coppyash*
print	cópia	*cohpya*
probably	provavelmente	*proovarvelment*
problem	problema	*prooblayma*
profession	profissão	*proofeesow*
programme	programa	*proograma*
pronounce	pronunciar	*proonunciar*
propane/butane (camping gas)	gás de campismo (propano/butano)	*gaj duh campeejmoo (proparnoo/bootarnoo)*
provident fund	caixa de previdência	*kysha duh preveedencia*
prune	ameixa seca	*amaysha seca*
pudding	pudim	*poodeem*

pull (tooth)	tirar (dente)	*teerar (dent)*
pull a muscle	distender um músculo	*deeshtendair oom mooshcooloo*
pure	puro	*pooroo*
purple	violeta	*veeooleta*
purse	portamoedas	*porta mooaydash*
push	empurrar	*aimpurrar*
puzzle	puzzle	*puzzel*
pyjamas	pijama	*peejama*

Q

quarter	quarto	*cwartoo*
quarter of an hour	quarto de hora	*cwartoo duh ora*
queen	rainha	*ryeenya*
question	pergunta	*pairgoonta*
quick	rápido	*rapeedoo*
quiet	calmo	*calmoo*

R

radio	rádio	*rardyoo*
railways	caminhos de ferro	*cameenyoosh duh feroo*
rain	chuva	*shoova*
rain, to	chover	*choovair*
raincoat	impermeável	*eempairmeearvel*
raisins	passas	*passash*
rape	violação	*veeolasow*
rapids	cachoeiro	*cashooayroo*
raspberries	framboesas	*frambooayzash*
raw	cru	*croo*
raw vegetables	legumes crus	*legoomesh croosh*
razor blades	giletes	*geeletsch*
read	ler	*lair*
ready	pronto	*prontoo*
receipt	talão, recibo	*tallow, resseeboo*
recipe	receita	*resayta*
reclining chair	cadeira-cama	*cadayra camma*
recommend	recomendar	*recoomendar*
rectangle	rectângulo	*retangooloo*
red	encarnado/vermelho	*encarnardoo/vermelyoo*
red wine	vinho tinto	*veenyoo teentoo*
reduction	desconto	*deshcontoo*
refrigerator	frigorífico	*freegoreefeecoo*
regards	cumprimentos	*coompreementoosh*
region	região	*rejiow*
registered	registado	*rejeeshtardo*
registration document	livrete	*leevret*
relatives	família	*fameelia*
reliable	confiável	*confeearvel*
religion	religião	*releegeeow*
rent out	alugar	*aloogar*
repair	reparar/concertar	*reparar/consairtar*
repairs	reparações/ consertos	*reparasoynsh/ consairtoosh*
repeat	repetir	*repeteer*
report	relatório	*relatoryoo*
resent	levar a mal	*levar ah mal*

responsible	responsável	*responsarvel*
rest	descansar	*deshcansar*
restaurant	restaurante	*reshtowrant*
result	resultado	*resooltardoo*
retired	reformado	*reformardoo*
return (ticket)	ida e volta (bilhete)	*eeda ee vollta (beelyet)*
reverse (vehicle)	fazer marcha atrás	*fazair marsha atraj*
rheumatism	reumatismo	*rayoomateesjmoo*
rice	arroz	*arroj*
ridiculous	estúpido/ridículo	*eshtoopeedoo/ reedeecooloo*
riding (horseback)	andar a cavalo	*andar ah cavarloo*
riding school	picadeiro	*peecadayroo*
right	para a direita	*parra ah dirayta*
right of way	prioridade	*preeorridard*
ripe	maduro	*madooroo*
risk	risco	*reeshcoo*
river	rio	*reeoo*
road	rua	*rooah*
roadway	estrada	*estrarda*
roasted	assado	*assardoo*
rock	rocha	*rosha*
roll	pãozinho (sem manteiga)	*powzeenyoo (saim mantayga)*
rolling tobacco	cigarro de enrolar	*seegarroo di ainroolar*
roof rack	portabagagem	*porta bagarjaim*
room	quarto	*cwartoo*
room number	número do quarto	*noomeroo doo cwartoo*
room service	serviço de quarto	*sairveesoo duh cwartoo*
rope	cordel/corda	*cordel/corda*
rosé	rosé	*rozay*
roundabout	rotunda	*rotoonda*
route	caminho	*cameenyoo*
rowing boat	barco à remos	*barcoo ah remoosh*
rubber	borracha	*borasha*
rubbish	lixo	*leeshoo*
rubbish bag	saco do lixo	*sarcoo duh leeshoo*
rubbish, nonsense	estupidez	*eshtoopeedej*
rucksack	mochila	*mosheela*
rude	malcriado	*malcreeardo*
ruins	ruínas	*roo-eenash*
run into	encontrar	*aincontrar*

S

sad	triste	*treesht*
safari	safari	*safaree*
safe	seguro	*segooroo*
safe	cofre	*cofre*
safety pin	alfinete de segurança	*alfeenet duh segooransa*
sail	velejar	*velejar*
sailing boat	barco à vela	*barcoo ah vella*
salad	salada	*salarda*
salad oil	óleo para salada	*ollyoo parra salarda*
salami	salame	*salam*
sale	saldo/liquidação	*saldoo/leekeedasow*
salt	sal	*sal*

same	mesmo	*mejmoo*
sandy beach	praia de areia	*prya duh arraya*
sanitary pad	penso higiénico	*pensoo eegeneecoo*
sardines	sardinhas	*sardeenyash*
satisfied	satisfeito	*sateeshfaytoo*
Saturday	sábado	*sarbadoo*
sauce	molho	*molyoo*
sauna	sauna	*sowna*
sausage (preserved)	chouriço	*shooreesoo*
savoury	salgado	*salgardoo*
say	dizer	*deezair*
scarf	cachecol	*cashcol*
scenic walk	percurso turístico	*paircoorsoo tooreeshteecoo*
school	escola	*shcola*
scissors	tesoura	*tezora*
scooter	scooter	*scootair*
scorpion	escorpião	*eshcorpyow*
Scotland	Escócia	*eshcossia*
scrambled eggs	ovos mexidos	*ovoosh mesheedoosh*
screw	parafuso	*parrafoozoo*
screwdriver	chave de fenda	*sharv duh fenda*
sculpture	escultura	*eshcooltoora*
sea	mar	*mar*
seasick	enjoado	*ainjoooardoo*
seat	lugar sentado	*loogar sentardoo*
secondhand	segunda mão	*segoonda mau*
second	segundo	*segoondoo*
sedative	sedativo	*sedateevoo*
see, visit	visitar	*veezeetar*
send	enviar	*ainvyar*
sentence	frase	*fraz*
September	setembro	*setembroo*
serious, grave	grave	*grarv*
serious, responsible	sério	*sairyoo*
service	serviço	*serveesoo*
serviette	guardanapo	*gwardanarpoo*
sewing thread	linhas de costura	*leenyash duh coshtoora*
shade	sombra	*sombra*
shallow	pouco fundo	*pohcoo foondoo*
shammy	camurça	*camoorsa*
shampoo	champô	*shampoh*
shark	tubarão	*toobarow*
shave	barbear	*barbyar*
shaver	máquina de barbear	*markeena duh barbyar*
shaving brush	pincel de barba	*peensel duh barba*
shaving cream	creme de barbear	*crem duh barbyar*
shaving soap	sabão de barbear	*sabow duh barbyar*
sheet	lençol	*lensol*
sherry	xerez	*sherayj*
shirt	camisa	*cameeza*
shoe	sapato	*sapartoo*
shoe polish	pomada de engraixar	*poomarda di aingryshar*
shoe shop	sapataria	*sapattareeah*
shoemaker	sapateiro	*sappatayroo*
shop	loja	*loja*
shop assistant	empregada	*aimpregarda*

shop window	montra	*montra*
shopping	fazer compras	*fazzair comprash*
shopping centre	centro comercial	*sentroo coomerciarl*
short	curto	*coortoo*
short circuit	curtocircuito	*coortoo seercooeetoo*
shorts	calças curtas	*calsash coortash*
shoulder	ombro	*ombroo*
show	espectáculo	*eshpetarcooloo*
shower	duche	*doosh*
shutter (camera)	diafragma	*deeafragma*
sieve	peneira	*penayra*
sign	painel/sinal	*pynel/seenal*
sign	assinar	*asseenar*
signature	assinatura	*assenatoora*
silence	silêncio	*seelensyoo*
silver	prata	*prarta*
silverplated	prateado	*pratyardoo*
simple	simples	*seemplesh*
single	solteiro	*soltayroo*
single	individual	*eendeeveedual*
single ticket	bilhete de ida	*beelyet duh eeda*
sir	senhor	*senyor*
sister	irmã	*eermar*
sit	sentar-se	*sentar-suh*
size	número	*noomeroo*
size	tamanho	*tamanyoo*
skate	patinar	*pateenar*
skimmed	meio gordo	*mayoo gordoo*
skin	pele	*pel*
skirt	saia	*syah*
sleep	dormir	*doormeer*
sleeping car	carruagem cama	*carruarjaim camma*
sleeping pills	comprimidos para dormir	*compreemeedoosh parra doormeer*
slide	diapositivo	*deeapozeeteevoo*
slip road	entrada para a rodovia	*entrarda parra ah rodooveeah*
slow	devagar	*deevagar*
slow train	comboio ronceiro	*comboyoo ronsayroo*
small	pequeno	*peekenoo*
small change	dinheiro trocado, troco	*deenyayroo troocardoo, trocoo*
smell, to	cheirar mal	*shayrar mal*
smoke	fumo	*foomoo*
smoke	fumar	*foomar*
smoked	fumado	*foomardoo*
smoked dried ham, Parma style	presunto	*prezoontoo*
smoking compartment	carruagem para fumadores	*carruarjaim parra foomadoresh*
snake	serpente	*sairpent*
snorkel	máscara de mergulho	*mashcara duh mairgoolyoo*
soap	sabão	*sabow*
soap box	caixa de sabonete	*kysha duh saboonet*
soccer	futebol	*footbol*
soccer match	partida de futebol	*parteeda duh footbol*

socket	tomada	*toomarda*
socks	meias	*mayash*
soft drink	refresco/refrigerante	*refreshcoo/refrijerant*
sole (foot)	sola	*solla*
sole (fish)	linguado	*leengwardoo*
solicitor	advogado	*advoogardoo*
someone	alguém	*algaim*
sometimes	por vezes	*por vayzesh*
somewhere	em algum lugar	*aim algoom loogar*
son	filho	*feelyoo*
soon	já	*jar*
sorbet	sorvete	*sorvet*
sore/wound	ferida	*fereeda*
sore throat	dor de garganta	*dor duh garganta*
sorry	desculpe	*deshcoolp*
sort/type	espécie	*eshpess*
soup	sopa	*soppa*
sour	ácido	*asseedoo*
sour cream	natas azedas	*nartash azaydash*
source	fonte	*font*
south	sul	*sool*
souvenir	lembrança	*lembransa*
spaghetti	espaguete	*shparget*
spanner (open-ended)	chave de porcas	*sharv duh porcash*
spare	reserva	*rezairva*
spare parts	peças sobressalentes	*pessash sobresalentesh*
spare tyre	pneu sobressalente	*pnayoo sobresalent*
spare wheel	roda sobressalente	*rodda sobresalent*
speak	falar	*falar*
special	especial	*eshpessiarl*
specialist	especialista	*eshpessialeeshta*
specialty	especialidade	*eshpessialidade*
speed limit	velocidade máxima	*velossidard masseema*
spell	soletrar	*sooletrar*
spicy	picante	*peecant*
splinter	farpa	*farpa*
spoon, spoonful	colher	*coolyair*
sport	desporto	*deshportoo*
sports centre	centro de desportos	*sentroo duh deshpoortoosh*
spot (place)	lugar	*loogar*
sprain	torcer	*torssair*
spring	primavera	*preemavayra*
square	praça	*prassa*
square	quadrado	*cuardrardoo*
square metres	metro quadrado	*metroo cuardrardoo*
squash	jogar squash	*joogar squash*
stadium	estádio	*shtardyoo*
stain	nódoa	*noddooah*
stain remover	tiranódoas	*teer noddooash*
stairs	escada	*eshcarda*
stalls (theatre)	platéia	*plataya*
stamp	selo	*selloo*
start	começar	*coomehsar*
station	estação	*eshtasow*

statue	estátua	*eshtartooah*
stay (accommodation)	hospedar-se	*oshpedar-se*
stay (be)	ficar	*feecar*
stay	estadia	*eshtadeeah*
steal	roubar	*roobar*
steel	aço	*ahsoo*
stench	mau cheiro	*mau shayroo*
sting	picar	*peecar*
stitch (medical)	ponto	*pontoo*
stitch, to	coser	*coozair*
stockings	meias	*mayash*
stomach	estômago/barriga	*eshtomagoo/bareega*
stomach ache	dor de barriga/ estômago	*door duh bareega/ eshtomagoo*
stomach cramps	cólica	*colleeca*
stools	fezes	*fayzesh*
stop, to	parar	*parrar*
stop	paragem	*pararjaim*
stopover	escala	*eshcala*
storm	tempestade	*tempashtard*
straight	liso	*leezoo*
straight ahead	em frente	*aim frent*
straw	palhinha	*palyeenya*
strawberries	morangos	*moorangoosh*
street	rua	*rooah*
strike	greve	*grev*
strong	forte	*fort*
study	estudar	*eshtoodar*
stuffing	recheio	*reshayoo*
subscriber's number	número de telefone/ assinante	*noomeroo duh telefon/asseenant*
subtitled	legendado	*lejendardoo*
succeed	sair bem	*syeer baim*
sugar	açúcar	*assoocar*
sugar lumps	cubos de açúcar	*cooboosh di assoocar*
suit	fato	*fartoo*
suitcase	mala	*mala*
summer	verão	*verow*
summertime	horário de verão	*oraryoo duh verow*
sun	sol	*sol*
sun hat	chapéu de sol	*shapayoo duh sol*
sunbathe	tomar banho de sol	*toomar banyoo duh sol*
Sunday	domingo	*doomeengoo*
sunglasses	óculos de sol	*ocooloosh duh sol*
sunrise	nascer do sol	*nashsair doo sol*
sunset	pôr do sol	*por doo sol*
sunstroke	insolação	*eensolasow*
suntan lotion	creme solar	*crem soolar*
suntan oil	óleo solar	*ollyoo soolar*
supermarket	supermercado	*supairmaircardoo*
surcharge	suplemento	*sooplementoo*
surf	fazer surfe	*fazzair surf*
surf board	prancha de surfe	*pransha duh surf*
surgery	consultório	*consooltoryoo*
surname	apelido	*apelleedoo*
surprise	surpresa	*soorprayza*
swallow	engolir	*aingooleer*

swamp	pântano	*pantarnoo*
sweat	suor	*soo-or*
sweet (sugar)	rebuçado	*reboosardoo*
sweet (nice)	amoroso	*amorozoo*
sweet	doce	*dose*
sweetcorn	milho	*meelyoo*
sweeteners	adoçantes	*adoosantesh*
sweets	doces	*dosesh*
swim	nadar	*nadar*
swimming pool	piscina	*peeshseena*
swimming trunks	calções de banho	*calsoynsh duh barnyoo*
swindle	fraude	*frowd*
switch	interruptor	*eenterruptor*
synagogue	sinagoga	*seenagoga*

T

table	mesa	*mayza*
table tennis	ténis de mesa	*teneej duh mayza*
tablet	comprimido	*compreemeedoo*
take a photograph	tirar uma fotografia	*teerar ooma fotografeeah*
take	tomar	*toomar*
take, last	durar	*durar*
taken, engaged	ocupado	*occoopardoo*
talcum powder	(pó de) talco	*(poh duh) talcoo*
talk	falar	*falar*
tall	alto	*altoo*
tampons	tampões	*tampoynsh*
tanned	bronzeado	*bronzyardoo*
tap	torneira	*tornayra*
tap water	água da torneira	*agwa da tornayra*
taste	provar	*proovar*
taxi	táxi	*tarksy*
taxi rank	praça de táxis	*prassa duh tarkseesh*
tea	chá	*shar*
teapot	bule	*bool*
teaspoon	colher de chá	*coolyair duh shar*
telegram	telegrama	*telegrarma*
telephoto lens	teleobjectiva	*tele objeteeva*
television	televisão	*televeesow*
telex	telex	*telex*
temperature (weather)	temperatura	*temperatoora*
temporary filling	obturação temporária	*obtoorasow temporaria*
tender	tenro	*tenroo*
tennis ball	bola de ténis	*bola duh teneej*
tennis court	campo de ténis	*campoo duh teneej*
tennis racket	raquete de ténis	*raket duh teneej*
tenpin bowling	jogar bowling	*joogar bowling*
tent	tenda	*tenda*
tent peg	espia/estaca	*eshpeea/eshtarca*
terrace	esplanada	*eshplanarda*
terribly	terrivelment	*terreevelment*
thank	agradecer	*agradaysair*
thank you	muito obrigado	*mweentoo obrigardoo*
thanks	obrigado	*obrigardoo*
the day after tomorrow	depois de amanhã	*depoysh di amanyar*

theatre	teatro	*teeartroo*
theft	roubo	*roeboo*
there	ali	*alee*
thermal bath	banho termal	*barnyoo termal*
thermometer	termómetro	*termometroo*
thick	espesso	*eshpessoo*
thief	ladrão	*ladrow*
thigh	coxa	*cosha*
thin	fino	*feenoo*
thin	magro	*magroo*
things	coisas	*coyzash*
think	pensar	*pensar*
third	terço/terçeiro	*tairsoo/tairsayroo*
thirsty, to be	ter (estar com) sede	*tair (eshtar com) sed*
this afternoon	esta tarde	*eshta tard*
this evening, tonight	esta noite	*eshta noyt*
this morning	esta manhã	*eshta manyar*
thread	fiozinho/linha	*feeyoozeenyoo/leenya*
throat	garganta	*garganta*
throat lozenges	pastilhas para a garganta	*pashteelyash parra a garganta*
thunderstorm	trovoada	*troovooarda*
Thursday	quinta-feira	*keenta fayra*
ticket	bilhete	*beelyet*
ticket window, bank counter	guiché	*gueeshay*
tickets	bilhetes	*beelyetsch*
tidy	arrumar	*arroomar*
tie	gravata	*gravarta*
tights	collants	*collan*
time	tempo	*tempoo*
timer	timer	*timer*
timetable	horário	*oraryoo*
tin	lata	*larta*
tip	gorjeta	*gorjeta*
tissues	lenços de papel	*lensoosh duh papel*
toast (drink)	brinde	*breend*
toast (bread)	torrada/tosta	*toorarda/toshta*
tobacco	tabaco	*tabarcoo*
today	hoje	*oarge*
toe	dedo do pé	*daydoo doo peh*
together	juntos	*joontoosh*
toilet	lavabos	*lavarboosh*
toilet paper	papel higiénico	*papel eegeneecoo*
toiletries	artigos de toilete	*arteegoosh duh twalet*
tomato	tomate	*toomat*
tomato purée	puré de tomate	*pooray duh toomat*
tomato sauce	ketchup	*keshoop*
tomorrow	amanhã	*amarnyar*
tongue	língua	*leengwa*
tonic water	água tónica	*agwa toneeca*
too much	demais	*demysh*
tools	ferramenta	*ferramenta*
tooth	dente	*dent*
toothache	dor de dentes	*door duh dentsh*
toothbrush	escova de dentes	*eshcova duh dentsh*
toothpaste	pasta de dentes	*pashta duh dentsh*

toothpick	palito	*paleetoo*
top up	encher	*ainshair*
total	total	*tootal*
tough	duro	*dooroo*
tour	passeio (turístico)	*passayoo (tooreeshteecoo)*
tour guide	guía turístico	*gueeah tooreeshteeco*
tourist class	classe turística	*class tooreeshteeca*
Tourist Information office	agência de turismo	*ajencia duh tooreejmoo*
tourist menu	ementa turística	*ementa tooreeshteeca*
tourist ticket	bilhete turístico	*beelyet tooreeshteeco*
tow, to	rebocar	*reboocar*
towel	toalha	*tooalya*
tower	torre	*torr*
towing cable	cabo para rebocar	*carboo parra reboocar*
town	cidade	*sidarde*
town hall	câmara municipal	*carmara mooneeceepal*
toys	brinquedo	*breenkaydoo*
traffic	trânsito	*transeetoo*
traffic light	semáforo	*semafforoo*
train	comboio	*comboyoo*
train ticket	bilhete de combóio	*beelyet duh comboyoo*
train timetable	horário de combóio	*oraryoo duh comboyoo*
trainers	tênis	*teneej*
translate	traduzir	*tradoozeer*
travel	viajar	*veeajar*
travel agent	agência de viagens	*ajencia duh veearjainsh*
travel guide	guia	*gueeah*
traveller	viajante	*veeajant*
traveller's cheque	traveller cheque	*traveller sheck*
treacle/syrup	xarope	*sharop*
treatment	tratamento	*tratamentoo*
triangle	triângulo	*treeangooloo*
trim (hair)	aparar	*apparrar*
trip	passeio	*passayoo*
trip	excursão	*eshcoorsow*
trip	viagem	*veearjaim*
trip	voltinha	*volteenya*
trouble	dor	*door*
trout	truta	*troota*
trunk call	chamada interurbana	*shamarda eenter oorbarna*
trustworthy person	pessoa de confiança	*pessoa duh confeeansa*
try on	provar	*proovar*
tube	bisnaga	*beejnarga*
Tuesday	terça-feira	*tairsa fayra*
tumble drier	máquina de secar	*markeena duh seccar*
tuna	atum	*atoom*
tunnel	túnel	*toonel*
turn	turno	*toornoo*
TV	TV	*tayvay*
TV guide	guia de TV	*gueeah duh tayvay*
tweezers	pinça	*peensa*
tyre	pneu	*pnayoo*
tyre lever	desmontador	*dejmontador*
tyre pressure	pressão dos pneus	*pressow doosh penayoosh*

U

ugly	feio	*fayoo*
umbrella	chapéu de chuva	*shapayoo duh shoova*
under	em baixo	*aim byshoo*
underground	metropolitano	*metroopooleetarnoo*
underground railway system	rede de metropolitano	*red duh metroopooleetarnoo*
underground station	estação de metropolitano	*eshtasow duh metroopooleetarnoo*
understand	compreender	*compree-endair*
underwear	roupa interior	*roepa eenterrior*
undress	despir	*despeer*
unemployed	desempregado	*dezaimpregardoo*
uneven	acidentado	*assdentardoo*
university	universidade	*ooniversidarde*
unleaded	sem chumbo	*saim shoomboo*
urgent	urgente	*oorgent*
urgently	urgentemente	*oorgentment*
urine	urina	*ooreena*
usually	geralmente	*gerarlment*

V

vacate	desocupar	*dezocoopar*
vaccinate	vacinar	*vasseenar*
vagina	vagina	*vajeena*
vaginal infection	infecção vaginal	*eenfecksow vajeenal*
valid	válido	*valleedoo*
valley	vale	*val*
valuable	valioso	*vallyoezoo*
van	carrinha	*careenya*
vanilla	baunilha	*bowneelya*
vase	jarra	*jahra*
vaseline	vaselina	*vasseleena*
veal	carne de vitela	*carn duh veetela*
vegetable soup	sopa de legumes	*soppa duh legoomesh*
vegetables	legumes	*legoomesh*
vegetarian	vegetariano	*vejetaryarnoo*
vein	veia	*veya*
venereal disease	doença venérea	*dooensa venerria*
via	através de	*atravej duh*
video camera	cámara de vídeo	*camara duh veedyoo*
video recorder	gravador de vídeo	*gravvadoor duh veedyoo*
video tape	cassette de vídeo	*casset duh veedyoo*
view	vista	*veeshta*
village	aldeia	*aldaya*
visa	visto	*veeshtoo*
visit	visita	*vizeeta*
vitamin tablets	vitaminas em comprimido	*veetameenash aim compreemeedoo*
vitamin	vitamina	*veetameena*
volcano	vulcão	*voolcow*
volleyball, to play	jogar voleibol	*joogar volaybol*
vomit	vomitar	*voomeetar*

W

wait	esperar	*eshperar*
waiter	empregado/garçom	*empregardoo/garsoom*

waiting room	sala de espera	*sarla di eshpaira*
waitress	empregada	*empregarda*
wake up	despertar	*deshpairtar*
Wales	Gales	*garlesh*
walk	passeio	*passayoo*
walk	passear	*passayar*
walk	andar	*andar*
wallet	carteira	*cartayra*
wardrobe	guardaroupa	*gwarda roepa*
warm, heat	calor	*calor*
warn	avisar	*aveezar*
warning	aviso	*aveezoo*
wash	lavar	*lavar*
washing	roupa	*roepa*
washing line	corda de estender roupa	*corda di eshtendair roepa*
washing machine	máquina de lavar	*markeena duh lavar*
washing powder	sabão em pó	*sabow aim poh*
wasp	vespa	*veshpa*
watch, clock	relógio	*relogyoo*
water	água	*agwa*
waterfall	queda d'água	*kayda di agwa*
water ski	esqui aquático	*eshkee akwateecoo*
waterproof	impermeável	*eempairmeearvel*
wavepool	jacuzzi	*jacoozi*
way	lado/direcção	*lardoo (deeressow)*
we	nós	*noj*
weak	fraco	*frarcoo*
weather	tempo	*tempoo*
weather forecast	boletim meteorológico	*boleteem metrolojeecoo*
wedding	casamento	*cazzamentoo*
Wednesday	quarta-feira	*cwarta fayra*
week	semana	*semarna*
weekend	fim de semana	*feem duh semarna*
weekend duty	serviço de fim de semana	*sairveesoo duh feem duh semarna*
weekly ticket	passe semanal	*pass semarnal*
welcome	bem vindo	*baim veendoo*
well cooked	bem passado	*baim passardoo*
well, good	bom/bem	*bom/baim*
west	oeste	*wesht*
wet	húmido	*oomeedoo*
wet (weather)	chuvoso	*shoovozoo*
wetsuit	fato de surfe	*fartoo duh surf*
what?	o quê?	*oo kay?*
wheel	roda	*rodda*
wheelchair	cadeira de rodas	*cadayra duh roddash*
when?	quando?	*cwarndoo*
where?	onde?	*ond*
which?	qual?	*cwarl*
whipped cream	chantilly	*shanteelee*
white	branco	*brancoo*
white kidney beans	feijão branco	*fayjow brancoo*
who?	quem?	*kaim*
wholemeal	integral	*eentegral*
wholemeal bread	pão integral	*pow eentegral*

why?	porquê?	*porkay?*
wide-angle lens	objectiva de grande abertura	*objeteeva duh grand abairtoora*
widow	viúva	*veeoova*
widower	viúvo	*veeoovoo*
wife	mulher/esposa	*moolyair/eshpoza*
wind	vento	*ventoo*
windbreak	páravento	*parra ventoo*
windmill	moinho	*mooeenyoo*
window	janela	*janella*
windscreen wiper	limpa pára-brisas	*leempa parra-breezash*
wine	vinho	*veenyoo*
wine list	lista de vinhos	*leeshta duh veenyoosh*
wine shop	casa de vinhos	*carza duh veenyoosh*
winter	inverno	*eenvairnoo*
witness	testemunha	*teshtemoonya*
woman	mulher	*moolyair*
wood	madeira	*madayra*
wool	lã	*lar*
word	palavra	*palavra*
work	trabalho	*trabalyoo*
working day	dia útil	*deeah ooteel*
worn	usado	*oosardoo*
worried	preocupado	*preeoccupardoo*
wound	ferida	*fereeda*
wrap	embrulhar	*aimbroolyar*
wrist	pulso	*poolsoo*
write	escrever	*eshcrevair*
writing pad (squared, lined)	bloco (quadrado, pautado)	*blohkoo (qwardrardoo, powtardoo)*
written	por escrito	*por shcreetoo*
wrong	errado	*errardoo*

Y

yacht	iate	*yat*
year	ano	*arnoo*
yellow	amarelo	*amarelloo*
yes	sim	*si*
yes, please	sim, se faz favor	*si, suh faj favvor*
yesterday	ontem	*ontaim*
yoghurt	iogurte	*yogoort*
you (polite)	o senhor	*oo senyor*
you	você	*vossay*
you too	igualmente	*eegwalment*
youth hostel	albergue de juventude	*albairg duh jooventood*

Z

zip	fecho de correr	*feshoo duh coorair*
zoo	jardim zoológico	*jardeem zoo-oloojeecoo*

Basic grammar

1. Definite and indefinite articles – the and a

Apart from verbs and adverbs, words in Portuguese are either masculine or feminine with **o** or **a** being the definite article and **um** or **uma** the indefinite article:

	Singular	Plural	
Masculine	***o***	***os***	- the
Feminine	***a***	***as***	- the
Masculine	***um***	***uns***	- some
Feminine	***uma***	***umas***	- some

e.g. ***um homem/uns homens*** (a man/some men)

The definite/indefinite article, the noun, verb and adjectives all correspond to each other in terms of number and gender,
e.g. ***O homem cansado entrou no banco*** (The tired man went into the bank)

2. Plural

Adding an **s** is usually sufficient:

casa/casas	(house/houses)

Some nouns form the plural irregularly, such as:

cão > cães	(dog/s)
relação > relações	(relationship/s)
mão > mãos	(hand/s)
doutor > doutores	(doctor/s)
canal > canais	(channel/s)
hotel > hotéis	(hotel/s)
lençol > lençóis	(sheet/s)

3. Personal pronouns

In general ***tu*** is used for **you** when speaking to close friends, relations and children and pets; ***o senhor/a senhora*** (or ***você***) is used in all other cases:

eu	I
tu	you (familiar)
você	you (semi familiar)
o senhora/a senhora	you (polite)
ele/ela	he/she
nós	we
vós	you (familar)
vocês	you (semi familar)
os senhores/as senhoras	you (polite)
eles/elas	they

4. Possessive pronouns

These correspond to the object they modify:

o meu/a minha	(my)	***o meu amigo*** (my friend)
os meus/as minhas	(my)	***os meus amigos*** (my friends)
o teu/a tua	(your)	***o teu irmão*** (your brother)
os teus/as tuas	(your)	***os teus irmãos*** (your brothers)

o seu/a sua	(your/his)	***o seu marido*** (your/his/her/her husband)
os seus/as suas	(your)	***os seus filhos*** (your/their sons)/their)
dele	(his)	***a casa dele*** (his house)
dela	(her)	***o carro dela*** (her car)
deles/delas	(their)	***o neto deles/delas*** (their grandson)
o nosso/a nossa	(our)	***o nosso cão*** (our dog)
os nossos/as nossas	(our)	***os nossos gatos*** (our cats)
o vosso/a vossa	(your)	***o vosso pai*** (your father)
os vossos/as vossas	(your)	***os vossos tios*** (your uncles)

5. Verbs

The most widely used tenses are the present, past and future, and the three main verb groups are those ending in -***ar***, -***er*** and -***ir***, e.g.

falar	(to speak)	
eu	(I)	***falo***
tu	(you)	***falas***
ele/ela	(he/she)	***fala***
você	(you)	***fala***
o(a) senhor(a)	(you)	***fala***
nós	(we)	***falamos***
vocês	(you)	***falam***
as senhoras	(they)	***falam***
os senhores	(they)	***falam***
eles/elas	(they)	***falam***

Portuguese has two different verbs of being, ***ser*** and ***estar***, applying to permanent and temporary states respectively.

ser	(to be)
eu sou	(I am)
tu es	(you are)
ele/ela é	(he/she is)
você é	(you are)
o(a) senhor(a) é	(you are)
nós somos	(we are)
vocês são	(you are)
as senhoras são	(they are)
os senhores são	(they are)
eles/elas são	(they are)

e.g. ***O meu pai é médico*** (My father is a doctor)

estar	(to be)
eu estou	(I am)
tu estás	(you are)
ele/ela está	(he/she is)
você está	(you are)
o(a) senhor(a) está	(you are)
nós estamos	(we are)
vocês estão	(you are)
as senhores estão	(they are)
os senhores estão	(they are)
eles/elas estão	(they are)

e.g. ***A comida está quente*** (The food is hot).

6. Demonstrative pronouns

este/esta	this (describes a noun, e.g. ***Este livro*** This book)
isto	this (used alone e.g. ***O que é isto?*** What is this?)
esse/essa	that
aquele/aquela	that (more distant)

7. Negatives

In order to form a negative sentence, ***não*** is placed before the verb, e.g. ***Não falo*** (I don't speak).

Other negative forms:

ninguém	nobody
nenhum(a)	none
nem...nem	neither...nor
nada	nothing
nunca	never